The Traveller's Guide to the

Holographic Universe

<copyright>

First published 2017

Published by Forward Thinking Publishing Text © Neil Hillier 2017

The moral rights of the author have been asserted.

All rights reserved. No part of this book may be reproduced by any mechanical, photographic or electronic process, or in the form of a phonographic recording; nor may it be stored in a retrieval system, transmitted or otherwise be copied for public or private use, other than for 'fair use' as brief quotations embodied in articles and reviews, without prior written permission of the publisher.

The information given in this book should not be treated as a substitute for professional medical advice; always consult a medical practitioner. Any use of information in this book is at the reader's discretion and risk. Neither the author nor the publisher can be held responsible for any loss, claim or damage arising out of the use, or misuse, of the suggestions made, the failure to take medical advice or for any material on third party websites.

A catalogue record for this book is available from the British Library.
ISBN: 978-0-9934652-3-9

Acknowledgments

Thanks to everyone involved in making my story an amazingly fulfilling experience.

Thanks to Richard Sykes PhD for editing this book. Thanks to Ann Hobbs for helping to publish it.

Thanks to Lisa on https://www.fiverr.com/lisaarts for helping to format it.

CONTENTS

The Traveller's Guide to the Holographic Universe. — 7

The Dutch Adventure — 15

The Guru — 19

Around the world — 27

The Internet Cafe — 29

The Idyllic Holiday — 45

Multi Milionaire — 49

The dream resort — 53

New Acquaintances — 57

The shotgun wedding — 65

Mafia at the internet café — 67

Amazing Thailand — 69

Road trips — 77

The Fight — 81

The Lunatics — 85

The best road trip — 87

The Gift — 93

The Tree House — 95

The downward spiral — 97

The Fishing Park Adventure. — 101

The Nun. — 109

And one man saved humanity. --------------------------------------- 113

The "Sale" --- 117

The Hotel --- 123

The retreat --- 129

The night manager -- 131

The Honey -- 133

The giks --- 135

Return to village life. -- 137

Back to Europe --- 139

Finally home --- 143

The Traveller's Guide to the Holographic Universe.

It all started in Holland, where Ray first had the chance to spread his wings.

First, though, we have to understand something about Ray's past.

Ray came from a broken home. His mother died of cancer when he was 13. He was kicked out of home when he was 15 by a father who openly admitted he never wanted children, who then remarried a schizophrenic woman who tore the family apart. Ray's younger brother, who had Down's syndrome, was sent to live in an institution when he was 13.

Ray never understood the cold heartedness in his family nor accepted it. Sending a Down's syndrome child to live away from his family seemed wrong. Whilst he could understand that independent living helped them to develop, family visits were reserved mainly for Xmas and birthdays and that didn't seem right.

This was very much the preferred way of treating Down's syndrome people in the UK, though. Even when they grow into adults, family contact is at a minimum. They don't look after the old people much better, in many cases confining them to a residential home where family contact is also limited.

That always saddened Ray. He never agreed with that corporate system and would visit his brother often. He had a close relationship with his grandmother too, the mother of his deceased mother, who kind of felt responsible for him. She was a worrier and neurotic.

Quite understandable really, having survived the 2nd world war in which she had to rescue Ray's Mum from the front door, minutes before a bomb dropped on it. It can't have been easy surviving that and it clearly fried her nerves. She worked hard, though, and gave her 2 children a decent university education. Her other son also loved Ray, as did his 2 daughters who were busy in jobs they didn't enjoy. They, too, were quite neurotic and loved to lecture Ray on how he should be living. Ray loved them, too, but always found it so weary to have to listen to them lecture on how he should live. He could never summon the courage to tell them how he felt. He bottled it all up and it made him miserable.

There was always pressure to do things he didn't want to do. His father was a very clever man, too clever in some respects. Believing only in science gave him the stubborn and outdated opinion that his son was some sort of genetic clone and should therefore like the things he likes. So Ray was forced by his father to do things and when he voiced his opinion that he didn't like it or didn't want to, he was punished or condemned. It left Ray with a feeling that he wasn't allowed to express himself; his duty was to do as he was told. That's how it was back then in his youth.

Ray was sent to stay with foster parents when he was 15, kicked out by his father from the family home. They were a decent enough family and gave him a loving home. Ray's a sensitive chap, though, and intelligent too. But it took him a long time to get over the traumatic events that happened in his youth. He failed all his exams at school and ended up taking a boring job in a bank, something he didn't really enjoy much, but which he felt he had to do, based on the teachings of his family and foster family. They were of the mind-set; "Get a job, any job; you're lucky if you enjoy your job in this world".

Ray's foster mother would often remind him of the words his father had written to her when he was kicked out of the family home. "MY SON WILL NEVER AMOUNT TO ANYTHING IN LIFE". Whilst this

was extremely saddening to live with at the time, it would also prove a motivational force in some of Ray's decisions later in life.

Ray had treatment for depression from a doctor; he also saw a counsellor and a psychiatrist who did their best to help him get over the traumatic events of his youth. But none of them were really effective. The most common approach back then was to give drugs to suppress the problem. Ray took Prozac for a while, which didn't really work well either. He would often phone in sick to work. Luckily he had an understanding doctor who knew his Mum before she passed away; he would sometimes write Ray a sick note for a couple of weeks so he could relax at home and watch videos of his favourite TV shows.

This pattern continued for years. Ray had some relationships with women but most of them failed due to his lack of self-esteem. He drank a lot of alcohol too. That was one of the few things about working for the bank he enjoyed; there was always someone to go over the pub with him.

So that was Ray's early working life; suffering in a mundane job and going out to get drunk to relieve the pain of his existence that he didn't understand and felt quite confused and depressed about. Yet he was in the system that his family approved of; even if it felt wrong, he had done what they said.

He'd visit his brother regularly, often taking him out for a weekend or to visit their grandmother. Ray loved spending time with his family and it saddened him that his father had no contact with him for over 10 years.

When Ray was 25 he contracted glandular fever. It's also known as the kissing disease. He remembers well the woman he caught it off; she was another drunken encounter in a nightclub. Anyway the doctor told Ray he may not have any alcohol for 6 months. Ray had a big dose of the fever and was off work for the same amount of time. He was very low on energy and didn't feel like doing much. However this also proved to be a blessing because, during that time, the bank was still paying him full salary and he wasn't spending much of it.

When he eventually returned to work, he had enough money to put a deposit on a home. This was a good move because up until that point Ray had lived in a multitude of rented homes, moving on average once a year in a futile effort to find happiness. Most of the homes were quite run down and depressing.

Ray bought himself a really good top floor flat with 2 bedrooms for a reasonable price and the mortgage payments were the same as the rent he had been paying. This gave Ray something to focus on and he worked so that he could furnish his nice new home as he liked.

This, however, was still something Ray had been indoctrinated to do by his family and society. Get a mortgage and work towards paying it off. Whilst it gave him a welcome distraction from the mundane nature of his life, it was simply a trip into the material world. He ended up with a nice looking flat, though, that he could relax in and he also owned a fast car. But still, once the trip into the material world wore off, he was faced with the misery of his existence once again. It made him feel trapped and he longed for some adventure and excitement in his life. That's right, Ray felt like a prisoner.

Around that time a computer system was introduced in the bank. Even though Ray didn't enjoy his job much at the bank, he was good at it. He had a good brain and, when he showed up for work, he did a good job. He had worked his way up from filing clerk to assistant manager in charge of 30 people. When the new computer system was installed, Ray didn't think much about it at all. He'd never been that interested in IT. However then he started to meet IT contractors who would come to the office to work on the computer systems; most of those guys were earning over £1,000 per week. This appealed to Ray as it would be a great increase in his relatively low income and a good opportunity to pay off his mortgage.

Ray quickly set about learning computers. His bosses at the time were reluctant to let him work with computers because he was quite useful to them in the banking sector, something he wanted to move away from. Luckily Ray was good friends with the two men who were selected to work with computers; he played snooker and drank with them both. So when he had spare time, often after his duties were finished, he would go to learn from them. Firstly he played solitaire in order to get used to using a mouse; his computer knowledge gradually increased.

As luck would have it, one of the computer guys resigned and Ray was asked to take over his responsibilities. This was a good move for Ray. Computer support work involved less people contact and longer hours, sometimes working through the night. It was something he relished and enjoyed learning more about.

The bank encouraged their IT staff to study for Microsoft exams. Ray enthusiastically accomplished this and passed the exams on the first attempt.

To celebrate that success, Ray went to Holland for a long weekend with a couple of friends.

You must remember that at the time Ray was still unable to drink alcohol. So when he smoked his first joint and ate his first hash cake, he felt ecstatic and fell about laughing. He laughed and laughed all that weekend and into the following week too. He had never felt so completely overjoyed in all his life. In fact, on the day he had to return to work, he was still laughing when he woke up. He wasn't able to control the laughter and thought about phoning in sick to take the day off. The laughter seemed to stop but, when he showed up at work, the first colleague he saw made him burst out laughing again and he couldn't stop. It happened to be his annual review on that day too. He really didn't get along well with his bosses at work and when the manager said to him "Out of the 3 managers, I think I have the most respect.", Ray started sniggering and asked her for a pen and piece of paper. He drew a big graph on the paper with 3 small boxes at the bottom of the graph, one slightly bigger than the other. Still laughing, he said to her "Yes, I think you're right. Out of the 3 managers you have the most respect as represented on this graph. However, if you take a look at the top of the graph where I've drawn another line, this represents the real world and true respect. So out of the 3 managers you are doing the best but you have a very long way to go." Ray said this still laughing, yet with brutal honesty. The marijuana had given him the confidence to be honest; but it didn't go down very well with the manager, who just stared at him with a stony-faced grimace.

Ray left the bank shortly after that. You must understand that it wasn't meant for him any longer. He'd only worked there because that's what he'd been told to do by other people and he'd followed them. This was an important turning point in his life; he was finally starting to break free.

The Dutch Adventure

Since Ray had a Microsoft qualification, which at that time was highly valued in the IT industry, he had plenty of job offers. Most were from companies in the UK, but he'd also applied for a job in Holland. After that memorable laughing weekend, he was keen to go back, even if moving to another country did make him feel afraid.

Sure enough, an interview came up with a Dutch bank. Ray was flown over by the agency and everything went smoothly. After the interview, Ray was walking through the centre of town with the agent when they received a phone call from the bank, offering him the job. Ray was stunned and needed to make a decision quickly.

Then he looked in front of him and saw a small group of bars next to a canal with bicycles parked outside. He'd seen this in a dream recently and it helped him to make the decision to agree to take the job.

Things certainly can change quickly in life sometimes. One day Ray was in a mundane job in England and the next he was packing his bags to start a new life in Holland, where he would be earning a whopping

£45 per hour. A friend of Ray's drove him to the airport the day he left and during the journey Ray never spoke a word. He felt stiff with fear about what lay ahead of him.

Little did he realise, there was nothing to fear, as it turned out to be a rather smooth transition. The job at the bank was relatively simple and required a lot less work that his previous job. The Dutch colleagues were genuine and friendly. There was also a friendly group of expats working there from around the world that Ray befriended and would sometimes socialise with. All that and he could smoke joints which made him feel good. Life was going well.

The Dutch had a high quality of life. A lot of employees at the bank would opt to work a 4 day week. They could add this extra day to their holiday entitlement if they wished, which meant they would have over 90 days holiday every year. It made for a relaxed atmosphere at work, as many people were living enjoyable lives and had lots of free time. Managers were open and friendly, too. They treated the staff with respect. Employment laws in Holland favoured the employees and this made for a pleasant working atmosphere.

After a short stay in a guesthouse, Ray moved into a small apartment in the city centre. This new rented home would prove to be an important meeting place in Ray's life. The landlord of that building was a colourful and interesting character who was in his early 40s.

Tom was a tall man and quite well built; he had a round face with a small mouth and had short hair. When he was 23, Tom became Holland's youngest millionaire after he introduced bar coding into the Netherlands. He got ripped off, though, by an American business partner and became bankrupt. He lost everything apart from one house that he'd forgotten to declare to the tax man. He'd used that house as collateral to buy the building in which Ray was renting an apartment. He kept one room for himself that he used as an office and sometimes as a place to sleep.

Whenever Ray came home from work, quite often Tom would be entertaining friends in his office which Ray would have to walk past to get to his flat. More often than not, Tom would invite him in for a glass of wine and a chat. Ray met some interesting characters there, one of which was a Tai Chi master. Ray enjoyed the stories they told and to his delight found that he was able to drink alcohol once again. Tom had invested in a guest house in the Czech Republic and would sometimes drive his Land Rover there, on the way back bringing crates of good quality Czech beer. Often he would have amusing stories to tell about how he avoided the customs officers, sometimes driving dangerous mountain roads to find a quieter border crossing.

Time went on and after a couple of years Ray was able to pay off the mortgage on his home. He felt rather proud walking into the bank to tell the staff he was there to clear all his debts. He'd accomplished what he thought was an important financial goal at the young age of 31.

He cut down on smoking joints because it was no longer making him happy; in fact it was making him feel paranoid and depressed. The same low feelings that he'd had on and off all his life came back to haunt him again and he found the waves of depression hard to live with. There were just so many questions about life that he needed answering.

That's when he decided to seek the services of the Tai Chi master, Sienna, whom he'd met through his colourful landlord.

The Guru

Because Ray was now a wealthy property owner, he could afford private Tai Chi lessons which he took every week in the comfort of his own home.

Sienna was an interesting character. In his late 40s he came from an Indonesian family which was a former colony of Holland. He had been raised in Holland, though, yet looked Asian. He had a big family with many children and lots of ex-wives who were still friends with him. A medium height man with a wide build and a bright face with prominent features that looked worldly wise.

Sienna would come every week to Ray's flat where he taught him Chi Kung and Tai Chi exercises. Ray enjoyed learning and found the exercises useful but didn't find that they helped him answer any questions he had about life. Sienna was very intuitive and saw that Ray was troubled. One day he suggested that Ray start to learn about the enneagram and the different soul types.

This was the start of Ray's spiritual education. The enneagram is an ancient symbol that a spiritual teacher called Gurdjieff introduced to the western world approx. 100 years ago. It can be used to understand many things and the first thing Sienna taught Ray about was the different soul types. There are 6 main types and a seventh that was rarer. Sienna also explained that people are made up of 4 bodies; a physical body, an emotional body, an intellectual body and a soul. The enneagram shows us about the 6 different faces of the soul. When people are genuine it's because they are following their soul, doing as it wishes. Even if someone has a nice personality it didn't necessarily mean they were genuine.

Ray was fascinated. He'd never heard about such things before. He'd been to a Christian school and went to church, but most of what he learnt didn't make sense to him because it had been forced on him. What Sienna was teaching rang true inside him. It made his heart sing; so he carried on learning more.

Sienna suggested that, once Ray had learnt about the different soul types, he practise recognising them in other people. He explained that when we look for the soul in others, we are looking for their good and can get a better contact with people. He did warn, though, that there are people in this world who are very egoistic and detached from their soul. He described the ego as the body, emotions and intellect. He taught that the ego should be used for good and for the benefit of humanity by listening to the soul; the soul reincarnated over and over, mostly into the same family.

Whilst Ray was interested to learn more, he was also a bit doubtful. There was very little knowledge about this available elsewhere. He read some of Gurdjieff's books and Ouspensky's Fourth Way, but it didn't tell very much about the enneagram and the types that Sienna was talking about. Apparently you had to study at a Gurdjieff school to learn that. Sienna had studied there but he found it tiresome: after a short while he had learned all he needed to set up his own system in conjunction with the Tai Chi he also taught.

Ray pressed on with it anyway. He found the knowledge of having a soul that reincarnated to be of great comfort, as it helped to ease the pain of his Mum's death. It also helped to explain some of his father's behaviour. One of the essence types from the enneagram had a tendency to be insensitive; these were known as the jovials. Sienna was also a jovial and exhibited similar characteristic at times.

Jovials also love to teach, talk a lot, show off and be the centre of attention.

Jovials are also very intuitive people and Sienna was a master at this. He intuitively knew about certain things and it was so fast. He explained that the spirit knows in less than a millisecond whilst clicking his fingers. For the mind it takes longer. Sienna was sharp, really fast and the things he had to say were so meaningful.

Sienna helped Ray to realise his own soul type; moon. He said of this type "moon feels the pain of this world". They are sensitive people and feel a lot. They can even feel what others are feeling sometimes.

There were times when Ray thought it was all a bit far-fetched. The ability to feel someone else's emotions sounded bizarre. That seemed to be the stuff of dreams or movies to Ray. That's when they started the energy lessons; of course Sienna intuitively knew these were necessary in order for Ray to understand.

During those lessons Ray learned about the 7 chakras of the energy body. They practised sending and receiving energy from them whilst sitting apart. "Do it with your mind." Sienna instructed, "Imagine the energy flowing through the chakra like a beam of light". Ray played with it, imagined he was sending an energy beam and then he would change it to an intermittent beam. To Ray's amazement Sienna could see what he was doing. "How is that possible?" he thought to himself. It must be that the energy is real and, if the energy body is the same as the emotional body, then it must also be true that it's possible to feel what others are feeling.

"Understand your own feelings, feel them to the maximum so that you know them well and can then make the distinction between what you are feeling and what someone else is feeling."

This helped Ray to understand why he felt uncomfortable around large groups of people. He was feeling what they were feeling. It was all starting to make sense.

Sienna was providing Ray with an education that he needed. It was something he had never received in his youth, partly because of all the traumas he went through, and partly because such things were simply not spoken about. They never taught meditation at school; it was only praying to God. As Sienna pointed out, meditation is listening to God, prayer is talking to God – we get farther in this world by listening. They didn't teach much about emotions at school, either, aside from supressing most of them.

"Embrace all of your emotions" Sienna would say. "Each emotion has a negative and a positive side". Fear was the hardest one for Ray to overcome; too many times he had given into it. "Fear and Bravery are the same energy.", Sienna enthused. Ray asked if that meant they felt the same "No, not the same feeling but the same energy. To understand this, you must face fear, not run away from it and eventually you will experience bravery.". This rang true with Ray too; there had been odd occasions in his life when he had faced up to fear and felt brave as a result.

Sienna would emphasise how important it was to embrace everything about our emotions. He would say "Embrace your tiger.", which in the eastern world means our devil. He then told Ray an old story about one of the movements in Tai Chi called "Embrace tiger, return to mountain":

"There once was a monk who lived on a mountain and did only the good things, rejecting anything bad. He meditated everyday; yet no matter how long or how hard he tried, he could not achieve enlightenment. Then one day the monk descended from the mountain into the local town below. Once there he did lots of bad things, getting drunk, fighting, stealing, sleeping rough and then having sex with a prostitute. On the moment he came, he got his enlightenment and could return to the mountain to carry on his good work."

It was invaluable knowledge, although there is a big difference between knowing the path and walking the path.

One time Sienna took Ray and some other students into a wooded area outside the city. There he instructed them to take a dead piece of wood, think of something that made them really angry, then shout and yell as much as they liked whilst hitting the piece of wood into a tree trunk. Ray had a good shout and took out his anger on the piece of wood. They had to leave quickly, though, for fear of someone calling the police. The next day Ray felt very weak, yet his voice had changed; it was now a lot deeper - which shocked a couple of his friends. He went to see Sienna who explained that the previous day's lesson about expressing anger in that way, leaves holes in your aura or energy body; which is why Ray felt weak and drained. A few simple chi king exercises had him feeling better in no time. Sienna then emphasised that the best way to channel anger was by putting the energy into your voice. He encouraged Ray to raise his voice to express his anger, as it was a much better approach than using physical violence. He also reminded Ray that the positive side of anger gives us the power to make things real or the power to do. So another good way to express anger was to do some work or exercise or compete in some sports.

This was a full and complete education Ray was receiving. It was all good knowledge that would help him to live a fuller life. Sienna would also speak about sexuality. In Holland this is taught from a young age at primary school, where children are taught to understand and respect their sexuality. There is very little homophobia in Holland, a stark contrast to England where it was rampant. Sienna encouraged Ray to have a homosexual experience to see if he liked it. Ray balked at that thought.

Sienna would often speak about the three universal laws for living. "We need food, clothes and a place to live. Everything else is secondary.".

Ray's contract at the bank was coming to a close. It had been a dream job and he'd made a lot of money. It was also time to come to the end of his education with Sienna and set off on a journey around the world.

Sienna talked a lot about the problems he saw in the world. "There's too much ego." he would often come out with "People needs to follow their heart and soul." he would rant. He also spoke a lot about the financial system in the world and how capitalism is no longer serving humanity well. "Most of the money is at the top of the pyramid now and there are many more poor people". Sienna, too, was poor but he lived a happy and loving life. His meetings were always colourful and with a loving atmosphere. There was always something to eat, drink and a joint to smoke.

During one of those discussions about capitalism Sienna said to a group of friends "If you give in a good way, you will get it back 50 times". Then he paused and said; "One of you must sell your home and do this.". Ray knew he was the one to do that, but it filled him with fear. That was one of his life goals that he had accomplished; owning a home was a useful asset since he was renting it out and had a regular income enabling him to do things. Still, if he wanted to face his fears, he knew he would have to sell it.

Ray was due to leave Holland after an enjoyable and educational three year stay. Sienna said on their last meeting "Don't believe a word I've said; go check for yourself and make your own story".

Sienna also warned Ray to watch out for black magic in Asia. He told about his father, who was Indonesian, and used to enjoy fighting a lot. He would go to a witch doctor and ask for a spell that gave him the strength to fight 10 men. He ended up dying a painful death. It was his karma; what goes around comes around. Ray was a bit uncertain about all that too but wanted to know more.

Sienna left Ray with the words "If all else fails, remember this: EVERYTHING THAT HAPPENS IS GOOD!".

Around the world

Ray had already travelled a lot around Europe, often hiring a car or taking a train away somewhere. Holland was easy to travel from and he enjoyed the trips around Western Europe.

So he started his round the world trip in Asia, Singapore to be precise, where he visited a friend and colleague from the bank in Holland where they used to work.

Richie was a Dutchman who had moved to Singapore to work in a bank as a DBA. They both shared a love of 2 things; drinking beer and Asian women.

It was in Singapore that Ray, through Richie and his girlfriend, met his future wife Lily. She was a Thai lady working in Singapore as a Thai dancer. She liked to drink, party a lot, had a good sense of humour, was straight talking and genuine. Since Ray was able to drink again it was a match made in heaven.

He carried on with his round the world trip, but used it up quickly so that he could return to be wlth Lily and live with her in Thailand. It was an enjoyable trip, though, during which he read a lot of good books that Sienna had recommended such as: Zen and the Art of Motorcycle Maintenance, the Carlos Castaneda series of books, Gurdjieff and Ouspensky. He wasn't so interested in visiting tourist attractions, though; he was more interested in observing people and talking with some about what he had learned from Sienna.

The Internet Cafe

Ray decided on an internet cafe in Bangkok as the first business adventure.

It was relatively easy to get. He saw an advert in a magazine and, after checking it out and the surrounding area, Ray and Lily took over an existing business.

Opening a business in Thailand was very easy. It took just one afternoon at the local government building to register the business and get the necessary licenses that cost next to nothing.

The cafe wasn't in a tourist area, but it wasn't too far from central Bangkok in the eastern side and near the university quarter.

Ray was excited because this was something his heart desired. He loved Thailand and knew that having a business like this would mean he could meet some interesting people. He had taken over an existing business with all the stock. All the computes were already there, wired up and ready to go.

Life was good at the internet cafe; many customers were from the nearby university quarter of Bangkok and the nearby African quarter. There were also a few Westerners who were living in that area, including another American family who had fled the USA after 9/11 and were living in a pokey flat next to the internet café.

They opened every day for over 12 hours. Running it was fun and, since Ray had worked with computers for several years already, he felt quite comfortable using and maintaining them. He also enjoyed teaching Lily how to operate them; Lily was quite thrilled to become a business owner. Ray installed a lot of free games on the computers and they had licensed versions of popular online games. Ray noticed that Thai people loved playing games and would often play the small computer games he had installed, as well as other popular online games. In fact, around that time the government came up with a new rule stating that children were not allowed to play online games after 10pm.

The shop was located on a busy main road with 6 lanes of traffic. Outside the shop was a large terrace where they put up some tables and chairs. This was used as a social area, somewhere for people to sit and talk. Ray and Lily would often end up having a good drink with their new friends. There were food vendors nearby and down the road was a supermarket that sold beer. Life was very easy there.

Good food was readily available which was freshly cooked up in minutes and they were never short of beer, wine or whisky. In fact the local supermarket offered a wide variety of imported booze and they enjoyed trying saki and other rice wines.

They often enjoyed sitting outside the cafe. Sometimes Lily would cook up a big pot of Thai food and sell that. Most evenings they would drink some beers with their customers and neighbours. Next door was a print shop run by a young Thai man. This later got taken over by an artist who opened his gallery there; and on the other side was a Thai couple running a karaoke bar – a place they would often frequent. They sold very nice food, too, which could be delivered. Thai karaoke bars are one of the preferred places for locals to unwind and enjoy themselves. In the same way some people in the UK unwind at a pub.

Two of their regular clients were Brits. Vic from Manchester was in his 70s and had retired to live in Thailand, renting an apartment in a block next door. He was a former soldier and had also worked in the bar business. The other guy, Matt, was Ray's age, came from Limerick in Ireland. He too was a former soldier and self-employed plumber. Both these guys had Thai girlfriends. Matt, however, had fallen for the wrong type of Thai lady. She worked in a goldfish bowl type massage parlour. She took all his money and then he learned she was already married. He'd sold his car too. Matt was depressed and Ray spent a lot of time listening to him and trying to cheer him up.

One of their Thai regulars was a colourful Thai man called Tric, who was a limousine driver. He was quite clever, having been educated in Japan. He was very outspoken and always had something interesting to say about politics. He was often on the phone to a local radio station giving his political views. He knew a lot of people too; one of his friends was a famous TV comedian.

Around that time a new prime minister had just come to power. He promised to wipe out corruption and help the poor. Lily was quite keen on this notion, as was Ray.

The previous owners of the internet cafe had warned them that they had been paying the police because they made a mistake with some software licenses and had a heavy fine to pay - which they had been doing monthly. Ray checked all the licenses they had and found them to be in order. So when the local police showed up demanding their payment, they refused to pay. At first it was only one policeman and he didn't like it one bit, raising his voice and wagging his finger at them. "Don't you dare make any mistakes." he yelled as he rode off on his motorbike. It was all rather scary. Lily told Ray that many Thai people called the Thai police "mafia in uniform" or "snakes" because most of them simply could not be trusted. It's quite simple really; they were underpaid and many would use their position of power to make more money. Police in Thailand carry guns.

A few days later, when they were open quite late, a group of undercover police showed up at the internet cafe. They were shouting and scaring them, yelling that they were open too late and would have to pay a heavy fine. They told them that each computer they had on would cost them 4,000 baht each. Since they had 12 computers this was indeed a big fine, close to a thousand pounds, and the truth of the matter was that they hadn't done anything wrong.

In Thailand at that time it was permitted to open an internet cafe 24 hours if you wanted to.

Anyway, as fate would have it, the next moment the door opened and in came Lily's best friend, Bee. It just so happened that Bee was the mia noi (2nd wife) of a high ranking police colonel in Bangkok. She quickly phoned him and passed the phone to one of the undercover police. Not long after that they left. Lily gave them a couple of hundred baht (about 5 pounds) so that they didn't lose face completely. They were never troubled by the local police again.

They were thankful to Bee and later on met Colonel Bard who turned out to be a useful ally in Bangkok. He was well educated and had a good sense of humour. They would give him a nice bottle of whisky every year in exchange for his protection.

It was like that in Thailand. You needed some protection from someone in a position of authority in case of any problems. Some foreigners preferred to have a good lawyer and would pay a small fee yearly to keep them on retainer. Having the protection of a police colonel was also useful.

There were a couple of times when Ray had been stopped by the police whilst driving in Bangkok. Since he was somewhat green then, they could tell and demanded large sums of money from him for running a red light or speeding. A quick phone call to Bard, though, would solve the matter.

Bard was good fun too; he would sometimes show up at the shop and drink some whisky with them. One afternoon, after a good drink with him, Ray needed to go out to buy some ink for the printer. "Hey borrow my car" said Bard, casually passing him the keys. This was not the first time a high ranking official had offered him his car. He was astounded but politely declined the offer because he was rather drunk at the time. It still impressed him how open hearted they were – no worries about insurance or the fact that he was drunk.

Truly amazing how laid back they were about certain things.

About mia nois (2nd wives). Ray learned this was something common in Thailand. A similar thing in the UK would be mistress or lover; only it was much more socially acceptable in Thailand. There, the more wealthy or powerful would have a 2nd wife. There were also giks too. Giks were more of a casual love affair, something that was growing with popularity in Thailand.

Lily and Ray both frowned upon the idea of giks but, deep down, the devil inside Ray quite liked it.

Ray noticed that Thais had their own view on the human condition. Just looking around Bangkok, there were lots of massage parlours that offered sex, too, and these were frequented by locals as well as foreigners and largely accepted by society. It all seemed a bit seedy. Yet, when he recalled his days living in Holland, there was also, at that time, a red-light district in most towns and cities. The Thais made allowances in their society for people to play around.

Ray had promised himself that he would delve some more into the Thai mindset. It was something he found fascinating and wanted to learn more about. It was no easy task, though, as Thai people can be very wily and don't give up their secrets easily. Sienna had warned him to watch out for black magic in Thailand, Ray was curious about this too.

One afternoon Ray was sitting outside the internet cafe with Noon, who was a lovely young university student, and withTric and Lily.

They started telling him about a religious festival held in the north eastern provinces of Thailand. It involved people allowing themselves to be possessed by spirits for the day. During this time they had no knowledge or memory of what happened and they willingly gave their bodies up for this period of time. Sometimes the spirits would consume whole bottles of whisky and it would have little effect on the bodies they had possessed. Ray was transfixed by this and wondered if they were winding him up, just making up a story to keep the foreigner amused; but they seemed very serious about it.

However, when Ray pressed them some more on it, asking more questions to find out more information, they all clammed up and looked at him stony faced. It was all rather bizarre.

Ray would share with them and other customers the knowledge he learnt in Holland from Sienna. They seemed to find this interesting, too, but preferred to stick to their beliefs. Tric would laugh, wave his hand and say "I don't believe or belong.". The Thais did share a similar belief that Sienna had once taught Ray – food, clothes and a place to live were the primary things we need to live. Well, the Thais had four primary things, the first three were the same and they also had a fourth which was medicine. Sienna immediately said "That's because they are sick." when Ray later told him about this.

It was a good learning experience and they were making new friends. One weekend they closed the shop and Tric drove them to Lily's home town to meet her family. They took another of their Thai customers with them.

Lily's home town was a small farming village. This was Ray's first time to visit and he wasn't made to feel welcome. It felt as if a lot of the neighbours saw him as a meal ticket and demanded cigarettes and booze. He felt extremely uncomfortable with the situation. Lily had three older brothers. Two of them were decent hard working farmers, the other one was an unruly alcoholic. Apparently he was broken hearted from a failed relationship with a woman. He was, by all accounts, very well educated, a qualified teacher and painter; yet to look at him, his shabby, scrawny appearance made him look like Gollum from the Lord of the Rings films.

Ray found the whole scenario bizarre. The living conditions in the village were very basic, just a wooden bench on the ground floor of the wooden hut and upstairs a large room with no furniture and a separate bedroom with a double bed inside. Out the back was a filthy looking kitchen area with fridge, gas cooking stove and a bathroom to the rear. A very basic bathroom which housed a trough filled with water and a plastic bowl to scoop the cold water out to wash with and a hole in the floor for a toilet. It was like something out of a museum. Ray couldn't even contemplate what it must've been like growing up in a place like that and was quite appalled at the living conditions.

Lily had a sister who walked with a limp; she did all the cooking and cleaning for the family and looked hard done by.

Ray couldn't wait to leave.

That was Ray's first impression of the place – barbaric – but he later learned to appreciate the simplicity of it all.

Most of that weekend was spent drinking. It was nice to get back to Bangkok. Ray was used to basic necessities such as a toilet he could sit down on, running hot water, a bit of privacy, internet and TV.

Ray couldn't get that trip to the village out of his head, though, and told his 2 British friends Vic and Matt all about it. Neither of them had been to visit their partners' homes and they were curious to know how he'd got on. Ray was painfully honest with them both as he recounted the moment when it all got a bit too much, being surrounded by all those Thai farmers who had their hands out demanding cigarettes or booze. He had left the room and went to lay on a hammock in the garden. He closed his eyes and pretended to sleep to escape from all the mayhem. Then one of the Thai men tried to wake him up by biting his big toe! Ray raised his leg, about to kick him, when the farmer smiled and wagged his finger at him. It was not an enjoyable initiation. They smoked all his cigarettes and he bought them crates of beer – It seemed like they would've taken the shirt off his back too.

Little did Ray know, though, he'd broken a whole bunch of important Thai cultural rules during that trip; hence his mistreatment. Well that, plus his age - he was quite young. Living in Thailand as an expat becomes easier the older you are, because Thais respect their elders.

Vic did not like the sound of it. However a short while later he braved the trip to his Thai girlfriend's village where he was warmly welcomed. The way he described it sounded like they rolled out the red carpet for him. Vic was more than twice Ray's age, which is why he got well looked after. Even then, Vic still had a minor problem with the father in-law who he bought a nice bottle of whiskey for.

That bottle quickly got added to the father-in-law's private stash and he returned with a cheap bottle of rice whiskey to share with Vic. Quite understandable, really, and Vic laughed it off.

Rice whiskey, or lao kow as they call it, was one of the cheapest forms of strong alcohol. It was a clear liquid yet very strong, cost

£1 for a litre bottle and was quite rough to drink. Sometimes it was mixed with herbs and left to ferment; then it was quite a nice and healthy drink if you had one small glass, as Ray's father in-law did every day. On its own, though, it really was quite horrible and needed a mixer.

Their favourite tipple at the internet cafe was beer. Ray preferred beer Chang because not only was it cheap, it was also the strongest at 6.3 percent alcohol. In fact someone once told him that 6.3 percent is the strongest beer they are allowed to sell in Thailand.

But the folks at the beer Chang brewery did not monitor how strong each barrel of beer actually was. So some bottles could be stronger and some weaker. It all sounded so chaotic, which he noticed seemed to be the norm in Thailand. Ray didn't mind, though, as it made drinking beer Chang even more enjoyable, as each bottle had a surprise element to it.

The Africans were the surprise package at the internet cafe. Ray simply did not plan on meeting any Africans in Thailand, but he had moved close to the area they liked to live. There were a lot of burly African men who would come to the cafe. Some of them were relaxed and easy going, some had a big chip on their shoulder and would complain that the price was too expensive in the internet cafe. Many of them would ask for a discount and some promised to pay the next time they came – which they never did. They seemed to have an attitude that the world owed them something.

Lily and Ray were growing weary of their behaviour and one day Ray had a go at one of their supposed ringleaders, telling him how tired they were of his friends' behaviour. This was a big step for Ray; up until that point in his life he hadn't confronted people much, but, given his new found freedom and education, he felt like facing fear. The African did not take kindly to Ray's words and got confrontational about it, not physically, just shouting a lot. Ray called him stupid and he stormed off. Later on that evening the burly African returned with a group of his African friends. It looked like the heavy mob was descending on the internet cafe, with all these muscle-bound Africans slowly marching in. They sat at the table and the ringleader started shouting again. As fate would have it, Tric showed up, as did a couple of his Thai friends and they sat next to Ray. Tric said Ray was their friend and they knew some powerful people in Thailand who could get them into trouble. It was a bit like gang warfare and Ray's side was winning, because, even though the Thais were a lot smaller than the Africans, it was their country. The Africans backed down; they shook hands and drank some beer together. They got along well after that confrontation.

Ray told them about the enneagram and one of the ringleaders smiled and said Africans represented Mars as the essence type.

These are the competitors, the ones with the most aggression and they love to reach their goals. Sienna had taught Ray that a good way to know someone well was to have a dispute with them "Check the condition of their tiger".

Ray felt relieved and was quite glad things didn't turn violent, because Thais can be extremely hot headed and most of them carry a weapon of some sort, usually a knife or a gun. Tric had a gun; one day Ray saw him in a very angry mood, marching down the street and stuffing a gun in his belt.

Another time in the internet cafe Vic got into a bit of trouble with some unruly drunk Thai men. They fired a gun near him which just missed, but the ricochet grazed his neck and he was taken to hospital.

They were all on a learning curve and, after events like that, quickly learned not to get involved in any fights. Not even to interfere if someone was taking an unfair beating, which sometimes happened.

Some of the Africans would come to drink and chat with them. Quite a few of them had businesses there and were making a living. They had a hard time because of their skin colour and their smell. A lot of the African men stank of body odour. Apparently the African women find it attractive but the Thais, who are very clean people, found it offensive. That, plus the Thai belief that the lighter your skin, the more respect you got, made the African's stay even more difficult.

Thai people took skin colour very seriously and many would spend a fortune on skin whitening products. Sometimes it appeared as if the police were picking on the Africans; they got picked up a lot. Their naturally confrontational attitude didn't help them much either, given that the Buddha had said to show anger was bad; this only antagonised the Thais even more.

Ray was starting to see the side of Thailand that you don't ordinarily see as a tourist and it could be shocking, scary yet also exciting, uplifting and he felt alive.

Sometimes there were accidents on the busy main road outside the internet cafe. One night Ray was drinking some beer with Lily and Matt when suddenly they heard a loud screech and bang. A Thai man on a motorbike had been knocked out unconscious and good old Matt put him in a taxi and took him to the local hospital. You have to be careful in some private hospitals, though, if you are being the good Samaritan. They may end up charging you if the injured party has no insurance or money.

Another time a Thai man had been killed instantly and they watched in horror as people appeared out of nowhere to quickly take his wallet and any other valuables. When you consider the extreme gap between rich and poor in Thailand it was understandable, but it was still quite a sight to see.

There was an extreme poverty gap too, in the road behind the internet cafe. Here there was a shanty town – a square kilometre of run down very basic wooden shacks. They would sometimes go there to play snooker on a worn out table in one of the wooden shacks. It was a very poor area, yet the people still had a happy-go-lucky attitude about them. Whilst playing snooker there, they had to be careful where they put their feet, so as not to fall through the rotten floorboards.

Some people say Thailand is the land of extremes. Seeing that shanty town, and then on the next road a luxury office block, was a good example of that.

One night there was a huge fire at the shanty town and it was all burnt down to make way for a new office development. Nobody ever said if it was an accident or deliberate. There were other incidents like this that left a mysterious and disturbing feeling.

Ray always felt safe in Bangkok, though. They would often go out late at night after closing the internet cafe. There were plenty of places to go to, because Bangkok really comes alive at night. There was a 24 hour snooker club nearby that they would enjoy going to with friends. Snooker is popular in Thailand and in the clubs there would always be a beautifully dressed Thai lady racking up the balls for each game. It was also possible to order food in these clubs and in some clubs it was possible to pay to take the lady to a private room upstairs for some adult fun. Whenever Ray heard of things like this, he often did a double take "They're allowed to do that?!". Ray was learning that the Thais delighted in their manipulative ways. He could appreciate it to because, whenever he spent time with Thai people, they were so happy most of the time.

Other times they would go to one of the popular tourist areas to visit a night market or to play some pool and drink some beer. There were plenty of nice restaurants to choose from and sometimes they would end up partying all night at a disco.

A short walk from the internet cafe was an old hotel that had been converted into apartments. It had a large rooftop swimming pool that for a small fee they could use.

Life was very easy in Thailand as an expat. You didn't need to be a member of the snooker clubs in order to play, nor with the swimming pool down the road. You simply showed up, paid a bit of money and could enjoy their services. It made for a nice relaxed feeling.

The most awkward thing was the visa. Ray was staying on a tourist visa, just like Vic and Matt, and it meant they had to leave the country every 3 months to get another one. Cambodia was the nearest border crossing and was the one they used the most. It was dodgy, though, and the border crossing was not a nice place to be.

There were stories about people being robbed there. There was a huge market and in the no-man's land between the 2 countries were a few casino hotels. They would stay in one of those hotels for a night or two whilst their passports were sent off to get a new visa. It wasn't too bad; the hotel rooms were a good standard, offering the usual air conditioning, TV and hot water. Food was OK, too, and there was always the casino if you like that type of thing. Ray would play a bit of poker but always put a limit on how much he would gamble away. Cambodia was very poor, though, and the border crossings are not the best places to see. Even though there were luxury hotels and casinos, the streets outside were basically dirt tracks with hords of grubby looking Cambodians going back and forth, some pushing heavy carts. Some were selling street food; Ray enjoyed the baguettes with a marinated pork and salad. There were groups of dirty looking children, too, that were begging foreigners for money. On one occasion Ray gave some money to one of them and was quickly surrounded by an entire group of miniature beggars who were pulling at his shirt. He later learned that this was a common scam in that part of the world. A lot of beggars worked for the mafia and were placed on the streets to earn money for their corrupt bosses. Ray became very selective about whom he gave money to.

Another alternative for a visa run was Penang in Malaysia. This was a longer journey by train through the south of Thailand but made for a nice change. A couple of nights in a guest house whilst they waited for the visa application to be processed, and then the long journey home by train. Train journeys in Thailand are very good, though.

They had air conditioned sleeper carriages, which were comfortable enough, and at each stop vendors would get on, selling food and the like. These were memorable journeys and Ray often met interesting travellers on the train. Malaysia had a much more solid infrastructure. Having been a British colony, you could see strongly made streets and pavements; the plumbing was good too. Ray didn't find the people there to be as happy and friendly as the Thais, though.

Laos was another good place to go for a visa. They have one of the best beers in Asia, hailed by the Bangkok post at the Dom Perignon of Asian beers. A lovely drop made of Bavarian hops, spring water from the foothills of the Himalayas, and Laos rice. The capital city, Vientiane, has a nice laid-back atmosphere. Quite a few foreigners have chosen to settle in this country, too. It was also very poor, though, and Ray and Lily didn't like the food as much as in Thailand. Ray also took the train to the Laos border, preferring the take 3rd class, which offered a reclining chair and a fan. It wasn't such a long journey as the trip to Malaysia.

Occasionally Ray would take the plane to Singapore to catch up with his good friend Richie and get a visa there. Sometimes he would take the coach or train back through Malaysia into Thailand.

The visa runs were actually quite enjoyable, as it gave a nice little break and Ray would usually get some good duty-frees on the way home. Travelling in Thailand was easy and affordable. In many cases there's no need to book a bus or train ticket in advance; just show up and away you go.

The Idyllic Holiday

On New Year's Eve Ray and Lily decided to close the internet café and take a holiday. They span a bottle on a map and it pointed east. Funnily enough they had heard about an island in the east that was developing into a popular tourist destination, so they decided to go there.

The journey was nice and simple. All it took was a short taxi ride to the bus station in Bangkok and then a long bus ride to the east.

Later, a ferry journey to the island and a short taxi ride to the main beach where they got off. It was a long journey but worthwhile.

Upon arrival at the island, it was if they had landed in another world and it cost next to nothing to get there. There was a lush rainforest that covered most of the island, beautiful beaches, clean air and what appeared to be friendly locals.

They had not booked a hotel and this was New Year's Eve, remember; but after getting out of the taxi they went to a small Thai restaurant to enjoy a few beers. The owners were very accommodating, phoning around a few hotels only to find they were all fully booked. It was not a problem, though, as the owner kindly offered them a room in her house for the night. Thais can be very good like that; a lot of them love foreigners and will invite them to stay in their homes.

That night they were taken by motorcycle to a secluded beach with just one bar and restaurant. It was idyllic; they drank and ate in the moonlight whilst seeing in the New

Year sitting on the seashore.

The following morning they were taken by their new friends to a resort that had a bungalow available.

Upon arrival they were greeted with a cheery "Happy New Year" from the owner, who was an older Swedish man. Lars was very tall with long hair. He spoke with a deep voice and had a good sense of humour. It turned out that Lars had been on the island for over 20 years and was one of the first foreigners to open a business there. He understood the culture well and was very laid back. "I don't do any work in Thailand, because I don't have a work visa" he smiled when his Thai wife asked him to pour a beer for a guest. This made Ray smile because he understood what Lars was talking about. In Thailand, if you are a westerner and want to work in your business, you should get a work visa. This requires a lot of paperwork and costs a lot. At that time you had to pay yourself a salary of £1,000 regardless of your earnings and pay tax on that. It was typically Thai in that they made it difficult for foreigners to stay in their country for extended periods; and they are strict about it too. Random check-ups by tourist police or immigration can prove to be awkward if you are working and don't have the correct visa – some foreigners have been thrown out of the country via a stay in jail for this. Fair enough, that's how the Thais like it; they are protecting their country and people in doing so. The easiest solution was to stay on a tourist or marriage visa and don't work too much, or do work that makes it hard to get caught. In any case, talking with guests was work, as was planning trips or events, yet could easily been seen as socialising.

Lars and his wife Mee would become good and trusted friends. They had a nice resort set inland on 1 acre of land with a few Swedish style bungalows and a large bar with a pool table.

They had a large dog that liked to drink beer. It followed them to a local karaoke bar one night and they got drunk together. In the morning the dog tapped on their bungalow door and looked at them as if to say "I've got a terrible hangover." before collapsing at the foot of their bed.

Multi Milionaire

Back at the internet café, Ray had decided that he wanted to move to the island and open a resort there. Lily was a bit hesitant. Being Thai, she knew that the islands in her country were run by the mafia. But Ray had his heart set on it and in the end she agreed to go with Ray.

He put his flat up for sale in the UK. It sold quickly and for a good profit on the price he bought it for 10 years earlier. A quick trip back to the UK to sign the necessary papers and then Ray transferred 11 million baht over to Thailand. He was now a multi- millionaire.

Now, what's that old expression? Ah yes "A fool and his money are soon parted". Well actually, Ray had in mind what Sienna the guru had said; "Give it in a good way and you'll get it back 50 times". So he believed he was being wise in spending it.

First thing he did was transfer 1 million baht to Lily, making her an instant millionaire. She was thrilled to bits. Ray felt good too; that feeling of making someone poor become rich filled his heart with joy. Then he bought a stunning condominium in Bangkok. It had previously belonged to a friend of Lily who needed to sell it to raise some cash. For 1.5 million baht he now had a luxury one bed home that was beautifully furnished with the best wooden fittings, nice lighting, glass cabinets, modern bathroom and a kitchenette with a bar area offering stunning views across the city.

Condominiums in Thailand offer a high quality of living. Within the complex of apartments there is usually a swimming pool, gym, car park, restaurants, coffee shops, min-marts, ATMs, beauty salons and laundries. Everything is provided for easy living; most of the businesses will deliver to your home too. The service charge in this particular complex was also low ; it worked out to be £10 per month which covered cleaning, security and maintenance of the lifts. Electricity and water were relatively low cost and there was no such thing as council tax or a TV license. In fact, during times of economic hardship, the Thai government reduced the cost of electricity. If you used less than 500 baht per month, it was free during the financial collapse in 2008. However, if you liked to use air conditioning, the monthly bill would be more than 500 baht. Ray, however, was happy using an electric fan and, if you can live like that, energy costs are low.

Condominiums in Thailand can be owned outright by foreigners so long as they are on or above the fourth floor. Ray, however, put it in Lily's name.

The history of the condominium proved to be somewhat alarming. Lily's friend, Sue, worked as a hostess in a Japanese karaoke bar. Her Japanese boyfriend was, at that time, stingy and didn't like to spend money on Sue. This saddened her. She also heard about black magic and, because she's quite easily led, she wanted to try it out.

Ray's ears pricked up at this point because he recalled Sienna warning him about black magic in Thailand. Sue went to see a witch doctor and asked for a spell to make her boyfriend spend money on her. The next time she saw him she asked for a new car and he duly obliged to her amazement. She had a very nice Toyota Sport-rider which at that time was a popular people carrier in Thailand. Then she asked for a new home and for it to be furnished like a 5 star hotel; hence the condominium.

A lot of Thais believe in black magic; that's what gives

it so much strength over there, according to Sienna. Ray gulped at the story of the condominium and doubted if it was really true. Lily was convinced, though, and said that most ladies working in the entertainment industry over there used it. It's something that Sienna used to go on about a lot – the power of belief; the more people believe in something, the more real it becomes.

At least they had a nice home in Bangkok, even if the back story was alarming. It left Ray wondering if he was susceptible to black magic or if he was immune. Sienna had always said to him "Nobody can do black magic or hypnotise you.". Ray liked to believe that; but his faith would be put to the test.

The dream resort

Ray was eager to spend the money on his heart's desire of a resort on the island. Lily was excited about it too. They'd enjoyed life at the internet café and met plenty of interesting people, but it wasn't enough. It had felt as if the flat back in the UK was holding him back and he was glad to sell it. A resort would enable them to meet more people and experience life on a paradise island. They talked about it a lot and Lily said she would prefer a place with a bar and shop: Ray just wanted a place where people could stay and relax and somewhere he could play pool.

So they made another trip to the island and returned to stay with Lars and Mee. The Thais they had met on their first romantic trip showed up to help them, after they made it known they were interested in buying a resort. Ray thought they were being kind but later learned that the unwritten rule on the island was that, for every sale of a property, a bounty of 3% of the sale price would be given to the person who introduced the buyer. Needless to say, because Ray had a lot of money to spend, there were quite a few Thais eager to help him.

They were taken around a few properties and after a while it became clear that they knew how much money Ray had to spend. He was quite annoyed because he'd made a point of keeping it secret. First of all he thought Lily had blabbed about it and they had an argument about that; but it later transpired she hadn't. Lesson learned though; the Thais know how much money you have, especially if you have moved it to a Thai bank account as Ray had.

One evening they were taken to a property that had a remarkable effect on Ray. It was, yep you guessed it, something he'd seen in a dream. It was more than that, though; it also encompassed all the things both he and Lily had talked about in their plans. It had a small bar, a guest house, garden and a shop. It was located in the heart of a small village; across the road was the beach and behind was the jungle. The place was perfect, just what they had in mind.

The owner was a local Thai builder, married to an American lady with 2 young children. He, too, seemed to know how much money Ray had and didn't budge on the expensive asking price. Ray didn't really mind, though; he was more focussed on living out his dream than the cost and he bought it anyway. There was a minor issue with the land papers, though. The owner had assured Ray that the papers were good, but he'd lied and it transpired that the ownership papers only held farming rights to the land. It was not such a big deal because they were still allowed to live there and they wouldn't have to pay any land tax; most of the other land in that village was the same. Ray was disappointed that the builder had been dishonest. According to the locals, he hadn't paid the 3% reward either, only handing over a measly amount to one of them who later had it stolen. Ray later learned that the builder had been beaten within an inch of his life whilst in America.

They were now the proud owners of a small resort on a holiday island. Well, in truth Lily was the owner, since Ray had bought it for her. The strange thing was, though, as soon as he'd paid for it, the magical feeling which he had, started to wear off. There just wasn't such a thrill about it now that it had been bought. He still felt good, though, and they went about altering the resort as they liked to have it.

Ray loves to play snooker and pool. The bar wasn't big enough to house a pool table but there was enough room at the front to build a small terrace. Planning permission was easily obtained from the local village head man and they recruited the help of some local builders who duly constructed a terrace which looked good. They bought a pool table shortly afterwards.

They made a few alterations to the guest house, which was quite basic when they first moved in. They installed air-conditioners, fans, TVs, wardrobes, hot water showers and good quality bedding. They had a wooden bungalow and toilet built in the garden. They made it very nice, a sort of "best of both worlds" combination. Offering comforts of the western world and set in the delights of a paradise island in the eastern world.

It was relatively easy running the business. Beer was delivered from a local store for the bar which would be the centre of their activities, seeing that they both liked to drink. Ray loved playing pool every day.

Life on the island was pretty quiet, especially during the low season from May til September. There were very few tourists around and it was mostly locals who would come to the bar. It was a good to start around this time, a nice slow pace and a chance to get to know the locals, who proved to be an interesting bunch from all over the world. Still though, the feelings they had as a tourist and now as a business owner were quite different. Gone was the thrill of being on holiday, replaced with the more down-to-earth reality of living and working there.

They found a lot of the locals were quite closed off and didn't seem interested in friendship at first. It took quite a while to win over their trust. It seemed segregated in that each business looked after itself. There was quite an air of competitiveness amongst some of the business owners, too. Many people would tell them to make friends with their guests; they would be their best friends. It dampened their spirits somewhat but they would end up meeting lots of interesting travellers.

The group of Thais whom they first met when they came to the island, who'd helped them to buy the resort, came one day to their bar and this time they were not smiling. "Thai people change." one said, looking decidedly miserable as he held out his hand and turned it back and forth. It left Ray wondering if he had some sort of personality disorder.

New Acquaintances

The previous owner of the resort had gotten into a German guide book. As a result one of their first long staying guests was a German man. Tomas was an elderly man who had lived a colourful life, living in America for 25 years as a farmer where he grew marijuana. He was an old hippy and had a great sense of humour. Ray, too, now had long hair and was easily adjusting to the laid back lifestyle on the island. Tomas had a Thai girlfriend and they would stay every year with them for several months. He was a jovial man and never seemed to get angry. He'd been holidaying in Thailand for many years and loved the country. He was also a bit of an expert on Thai culture, having read quite a few books on the subject. "They want to manipulate you." he would muse.

They made new friends with quite a few Brits who were travelling in Thailand too – Scots, English and Irish - who would stay at their resort and enjoy the freedom of drinking and partying all night long. Lily had learnt from a few guests how to make cocktails and these went down well late at night. Of these guests, one of the more memorable was a young Englishman who was the son of a wealthy insurance company owner in the UK. He drank and took a lot of drugs, seemed disillusioned with life and had little concept of money. Ray felt sorry for him, though, and trusted him to stay in the condominium in Bangkok for a short while.

Some Canadians were amongst their first guests too. Notably one Asian looking Canadian who was born in Cambodia and was evacuated to Canada as a child during the reign of Pol Pot. This was his first time returning home and he was scared to go. He'd gotten to the Cambodian border and turned back in fear. He didn't know what he would find or if any of his family was alive. A daunting prospect for sure.

The Canadians were a cheery and friendly group. Ray had once been to Toronto on holiday as a younger man and had had a good time there. It was quite fitting that he should meet up with some Canadians at the resort.

There were elderly French couples that liked to stay in the low season. They asked to use the kitchen to cook up their own breakfast; Ray and Lily were happy to oblige. Since they were opening the bar until late, they didn't get up in time to make breakfast. It didn't really matter, since they shared their kitchen with those who needed it and there were restaurants across the road and next door that offered good food.

The French had a historical connection with that part of the world, having colonised Cambodia which was only 50 miles away. There were quite a few French expats who had settled on the island.

Plenty of Swedes would show up; they really loved Thailand. Sometimes they were friends of Lars. There was one memorable young Swedish family. The lady said her husband was her knight in shining armour that came to rescue her from a bad marriage and helped to raise their daughter. Lily said the same about Ray. Lily too had a young daughter who was being raised by Lily's father, as is often the way in Thailand; the grandparents raise the children whilst the parents work and raise money for the family. Part of Ray and Lily's income went towards raising her daughter, who would come to stay with them during school holidays.

Ray was enjoying living out his dream, often playing pool

all night with his guests. A variety of Thais would sometimes show up at the bar and Lily would have a whale of a time drinking and talking with them. Thai people really know how to live in moment and have fun.

They are so animated when they do so. Ray used to sit in awe as he watched and listened to them talk and laugh. He wasn't fluent in Thai but could understand some of what they were saying and sometimes Lily would translate what they were laughing about.

Thai people seemed to make time stand still when they were enjoying the moment. It really was a sight to see and experience - the feeling of sheer joy and timelessness. Those moments were priceless.

Thais are a very polite and respectful people. They don't like confrontation either and in their society, if you have a problem with someone, you don't confront them about it; you tell one of their friends who will then politely pass the comment on. It took quite an adjustment for Ray to get used to, and what he found particularly difficult was the fact that his friends would know a lot about his personal life. It was something quite alien to life in the UK; yet that was the lifestyle in Thailand and it encouraged a strong sense of community.

When in Rome, do as the Romans do. This was also something Sienna had suggested – learn to live like one of them, embrace their culture and your life will be better.

Ray had befriended quite a few of the locals after a few months.

There was a Frenchman who ran a restaurant in the village. Pierre was one of the foreign pioneers on the island and had been there a very long time. He was quite eccentric and had a good sense of humour. He, too, said to Ray that it was best to live like one of the locals and found that, in doing so, he had more respect from them and felt like part of the family. He had a hard life, though. His mother was a prostitute and his father an alcoholic. Both had passed away. Pierre had two young boys he was raising alone. Their mother was Thai but had abandoned them when she left him. He was an alcoholic, too, often drinking whisky out of a coffee cup for his breakfast. Pierre was a good cook, though; he served up some amazing French meals and would tell stories about how the island was years ago.

Then there was an Arab guy who ran a scuba diving business in the village. He was extremely arrogant, though, and had been through his fair share of drama since he moved to the island. When he first opened, he moored his boat at the central pier in the village without asking anyone's permission. Shortly afterwards, he arrived one morning to find the locals had sunk his boat! He complained and was told "Who the hell do you think you are? This is our island.". He liked to drink in Ray's bar and would bring his colleagues and customers along too. The most memorable were 2 of his staff, a young English couple from Accrington. They were very open minded and easy going for such a young age.

There was an eccentric Austrian man who ran one of the busiest restaurants on the island and served up great international food. Ray made a good deal with him to have tasty pizzas delivered to his resort for a discount price. In fact, Ray made similar deals with quite a few restaurants in the village. Not only did it satisfy his own stomach, it meant his guests had a wide variety of food to choose from; and pizzas, which could be delivered up until 11pm, went well with beer.

Across the street lived an Italian lady who ran a successful Italian restaurant. She was a former air hostess and could speak several languages. She started on the island around the same time as Ray, as did some of the other neighbours, a Swedish lady and her Thai girlfriend from Bangkok. They were around Ray's age and got along well, having a good sense of humour and a love of drinking, especially the Swedish lady who was a big, butch lesbian.

Also nearby was a middle aged Japanese man who ran a resort roughly the same size as Ray's. Yomi was a martial arts expert and worked six months of the year in Japan as a manager. He looked and acted like Mr Myagi out of the karate Kid films and taught Ray and Lily some martial arts moves. Yomi enjoyed showing off his skills and one night in the bar a fight almost broke out between 2 tourists, unsurprisingly between an Englishman and a German man. Quick as a flash, Yomi disarmed the drunk German of the pool cue and pushed him so hard out of the bar that he didn't even look back; he just carried on walking. Yomi was a useful ally and it was comforting to know he was a friend and lived across the road. That said, though, there was hardly any violence in the bar.

Around that time there was the arrival of a young man from Denmark called Denis. He was a good friend of Lars, who jokingly referred to him as the son he never had. Denis, as Lars put it, was a phenomenon. He was full of life and very eccentric. He rented a small resort with a bar where he enjoyed playing air guitar and dancing around in his bar with loud rock music blaring out of his stereo. This was of some concern to the neighbours because it was, like many in Thailand, an open air bar and Denis would often start playing loud music at 7am whilst dancing around his bar pretending to play an invisible guitar. He was quite an attraction for those who like that sort of behaviour and his bar was often busy. He was well liked by many of the local Thais too.

There were many colourful characters living on the island. It made for an exciting life. Ray was reminded of a line from the classic film "Butch Cassidy and the Sundance kid" when they met the old mine owner in Bolivia and he told them that living abroad for 10 years "makes you colourful". Ray found that to be perfectly true about the expats he was encountering. Living in Thailand as an expat afforded people a lot of personal freedom; they felt comfortable to be themselves.

You never know who is going to walk through your door when you run a resort. That's one of the plus points. There was also a nice buzz about the place because it became abundantly clear that people were given a lot of leeway; yet it left Ray wondering who would step in if things turned nasty. It was a bit like living on a knife edge. There were lots of thrills to it but there was also danger. There were other expats that Ray gave a wide berth to, because they were into living out their dream of being violent or acting like a mafia.

Further afield on the island Ray made friends with the local vet who was an American Expat. Anne had previously worked as a scuba diving instructor and moved on to set up a volunteer veterinary clinic. She was also a special character, well travelled and had also lived in Africa. Anne told Ray that her cousin was a fireman during the 9/11 disaster in New York. He told her that he and many other firemen had heard explosions going off inside the buildings before they collapsed. This prompted Ray to investigate some more and he watched quite a few documentaries about that and other famous world events. That gave him, and any other guests who were interested, a different perspective on things. Anne liked to tell some scary stories. Apparently at that time there was no anti-venom kept on the island. So if anyone got bitten by a snake, you'd better hope it was during the day when the ferry was running to the mainland. Also, there was a poisonous centipede that was black and red in colour; apparently if you got bitten you became temporarily paralysed. Anne lived alone in a remote part of the island, next to the jungle.

Hmm, snakes. When Anne mentioned snakes, Ray felt really scared. There are a lot of snakes in Thailand, some poisonous, some not. On the island there were quite a few but they seemed to stay in the jungle. Occasionally you could see them crossing the road. If you were riding past on a motorbike you needed to lift your legs up. The most important realisation was that the snakes didn't want to attack people; it was just best to stay out of their way because they will defend themselves.

Anne's best friend was Lucy from Finland who, like Anne, could speak Thai fluently. She'd lived on the island for a long time, knew many people and owned a nice restaurant in the centre of the main beach. She was of great help to many foreigners, tourists and expats, who had run into trouble.

They certainly were a colourful group of expats.

The shotgun wedding

Around that time Ray and Lily got married in a hastily arranged wedding in her home village. They had their outfits made by one of the Nepalese tailors on the island. It was quite a culture shock, especially when Ray was woken at 6am to start the proceedings. He had been up all night with Lily and her family drinking the night before, so wasn't in the best of moods for the ceremony. They survived it, though, even if it was quite chaotic. Later on Denis and his Thai wife showed up; they, too, had got married earlier that day in the same province.

Mafia at the internet café

Ray and Lily made a trip back to Bangkok to check up on the internet café. They had entrusted it with Lily's younger brother, Bah, who was adopted by her parents after his father left him outside their front door as a baby. He was bad news but likeable, had been in and out of prison and other troubles all his young life. However, at that time he was the only family member who was available to help.

Well, the internet café was still running, it had all the equipment inside and a few customers when they showed up. A lot of the customers were not happy, though, as Bah would often close the shop and he wasn't very helpful. Ray found a huge sword hidden under the sofa in the shop; this was a chosen weapon for the mafia in Thailand, known as a Sparta. When Ray discovered that Bah had spent all the profits, hadn't paid the rent or any of the bills, he knew he couldn't be trusted and had to close the shop.

Ray had great support from Lily's family, though, who came in 2 pickup trucks on a long journey from their village. They took half of the computers to the village in one truck and the remaining half went in the other truck to the island.

At the village Ray donated most of the computers to Lily's family and one to the head monk at the temple plus a printer. In return the monk gave Ray a small framed picture of a monk smoking a cigar. Ray didn't think much of it and was about to throw it in the back of the car when Lily shrieked and stopped him saying "No,no,no". Apparently this monk was something of a big deal in Thailand and the picture he'd given Ray was of another famous monk. This was the only monk allowed to smoke cigars and he advised the King of Thailand. Lily saw it as something of a big honour, but it was a bit lost on Ray at the time. She hung it up behind the bar at the resort.

Amazing Thailand

Ray now had an abundance of computers and gave most of them away to some of his new friends on the island. One went to Lars in exchange for a supply of weed. This proved to be a very good deal because Lars was an honourable man and kept his word. Ray had a plentiful supply of grass to share with his guests for free. One went to Anne the vet in exchange for free animal treatment. Another went to the eccentric Frenchman, Pierre, for which he served up Ray and Lily a first class French meal with a good bottle of wine. It felt good to do these things and helped build the friendships.

Things were going well. They'd built up some good contacts and friends. It meant that when their resort was quiet, they could go and visit friends. It often involved a lot of drinking and occasionally smoking a joint but it was a lot of fun. Lars in particular had a great sense of humour and would speak honestly and genuinely about his experiences. "Sometimes they are totally out of order." he would boom out loud and then laugh about the Thais." They have no limit!" raising his arm to the ceiling, he said on another occasion. "You're young enough to make it again if you lose everything." he told Ray, after he'd learned Ray had given everything up. Lars had developed the ability to express his anger using his voice. Ray was most impressed by this as he recalled this was something Sienna had spoken about. He'd not been involved in any fights during his 20 years in Thailand, instead settling disputes simply by using his voice. Lars had built up his resort from nothing for his friends to stay there. He wasn't in it to make a profit, he was there for fun and it was a pleasure to spend time there. The Swedes loved it too. Lars explained that in Sweden alcohol can only be bought from government-run bottle shops. This explained why the Swedes liked to drink so much in Thailand. They were a nice bunch, though, and handled their drink well.

They'd discovered a lot of nice restaurants and would often eat out. The island offered a wide variety of cuisines from around the world and most at affordable prices. There were a couple of late night restaurants that they would frequent after closing the bar at 3 or 4 am, which was quite the norm for them. Sometimes they would take their guests with them and there would usually be other locals or tourists out at that time, There would be someone with a guitar and they would sing songs together, sometimes until the sun came up.

A typical day for them would start late morning or early afternoon. They had a cleaner who was from Cambodia who thankfully, by that time, had cleaned up the place from the partying the night before. Then they would open the bar mid or late afternoon. Inside the bar they had a computer with internet access. Ray would plonk himself down in front of that and do a bit of surfing and put on music most days when they weren't going out somewhere. Lily would serve drinks behind the bar. Guests would roll in and out of the bar throughout the day and night. Sometimes it was a local who wanted a chat and other times it would be a tourist wanting to talk or needing some information about things to do on the island. Some would stay all night to play pool and drink. It depended on the time of year and how busy it was. Mostly it was busy from December to March and the rest of the time it was pretty quiet; yet they always seemed to have guests in their bar, even if it was one or two locals or tourists.

After the first year Denis, the young phenomenon from Denmark, didn't have enough money to pay the rent on his resort for the next year. He'd blown most of the profits on enjoying himself. He had had some fantastic times, though. One night, whilst driving his motorbike back from a village on the other side of the island, whilst driving on the quiet stretch of road that went through the jungle, he crashed his bike, careering off the road, down a ditch and landed in the jungle. He stood up, dusted himself down and was completely uninjured, thanks to the copious amounts of alcohol and weed he'd consumed earlier. Then out of nowhere, a small Thai lady was pushing his motorbike towards him smiling and saying "Here you are, Denis".

He had no idea who she was or where she came from.

Another time he was doing his usual routine of playing air guitar in front of his guests late at night when a police car pulled up, the window was wound down and a serious looking police officer said "Turn your music off or go to jail". Even the police officer found it hard not to laugh. This gave some of his guests a funny story to tell.

Denis had fallen out with the Austrian man whose popular restaurant was nearby and when the Austrian's patience snapped one night, he hit Denis. This turned into a bit of a mini war and neither party was particularly forgiving. Denis later tried to burn down one of the signs advertising the Austrian restaurant.

It was probably a good thing Ray was going home; things had gotten a bit out of hand but he'd leave with many amazing memories, some good friends and a lovely Thai wife.

Ray agreed to take on Denis's staff, two party loving Isaan ladies who had worked for him as hostesses. Yep that's right; Ray had become a pimp.

They recruited another lady who came with a tourist and wanted to stay, so now there were 3 ladies working in their resort. They'd given them the bungalow as free accommodation, free food and whatever they made from customers was theirs to keep. They attracted a lot of single guys to the bar and business was good.

Lily was in her element and loving every minute being the boss, or mamasan as they are known in Thailand. It didn't sit easy with Ray, though, as that wasn't what he'd had in mind when he moved there. All he really wanted was to chill out and make some friends. A busy brothel was not what he had in mind when he first moved there. But, as Lily correctly pointed out, this was popular in Thailand, especially in the tourist areas. It made Lily happy, though, and that made Ray feel good.

Ray took more of a back seat and would spend more time inside the resort chatting with guests or on the internet in his room, going to the bar occasionally or out to visit friends. He taught himself to make websites and had some useful advice from other web designers living on the island.

They started doing day trips. It was something new and interesting to get involved in during the day. One of their German guests had led them into the jungle one day to show them a secluded rock pool. It took quite some effort to find it the first time. One of the jungle trekkers had warned them not to stray off the path but they were all a bit tipsy and wandered into an area densely populated by large spiders. Ray managed to walk head first into a giant cobweb which scared the life out of him and he frantically dusted it off himself. It looked like a scene from a comedy version of an Indiana Jones film.

They found the rock pool eventually though.

The rock pool was a lovely spot to get away from it all. It was possible to drive part of the way there too. Ray got permission from the landowner to drive his jeep along a dirt track that led to a huge clearing in the jungle where he would park up and walk the rest of the way to the rock pool. They had many good days out there and would load up the jeep with food and drink before heading off with some guests. If they were lucky, the elephant trekkers would show up and it was possible to swim with elephants in the rock pool. On the way home they would stop at one of the many nice restaurants on route.

They also arranged boat trips, sometimes in conjunction with Lars and his Swedish friends. The boat trips were equally impressive.

There were quite a few smaller islands in the vicinity and they would stop at one of those for the afternoon which gave the feeling they were truly living in paradise. Some of those smaller islands had some basic bungalows and a restaurant, all powered by generator. Some were uninhabited. One was populated entirely by monkeys. Another was used as a chicken farm. There were also nice spots to stop and do a bit of snorkelling. The water was so clean and clear. Since it was nice and warm it was a pleasure to go swimming in too. Lars would sometimes ask the captain to stop the boat in the middle of nowhere, just so people could enjoy jumping into the water. When the boat pulled into one of the smaller islands, you could clearly see fishes under the water and sometimes there would be some Thai guys in the water scooping up handfuls of tiger fish. These were memorable trips. On the way back they would stop at the fishing village where the boat stopped. Along the pier was a host of restaurants offering delicious, freshly caught seafood dishes.

They'd made some more new friends on the island. Most notably an older Canadian man called Paul who came from Montreal. He was well travelled and had been around the world in the 1960s when he spent a lot of time in India learning meditation from gurus in ashrams. He was an old rocker and had a lot of interesting stories to tell. He was quite forthright too and would speak his mind honestly. He had a Thai wife called Tao who was a jovial lady and got along well with Lily. Paul liked to smoke a lot of weed and drink whisky. His parents were deceased but they had both worked as psychiatrists. Paul was a very intelligent man with a lot of useful insights into life. He'd speak with Ray about similar things that he'd learnt from Sienna. He'd learnt from one of the best Indian gurus whom Ray later looked up on the internet and found that he had indeed given wonderful speeches to the U.N. Ray was absolutely fascinated to hear Paul's stories and opinions. About life he would say "Understand your past, make peace with yourself. Understand the choices you made, what happened to you as a result and what you learned from them." Paul also said that meditation was listening to God and prayer was talking to God. It was reassuring for Ray to hear these things; any lingering doubts he may have had about Sienna's teachings would dissipate. It was a genuine pleasure to meet the worldly wise Paul and they would become good friends. He didn't like it much on the island, though, and would soon move away. He and Tao moved back to an island closer to Bangkok that was more established and a lot smaller. They remained friends, though, and Ray would sometimes visit them.

There was another new addition to the island in the form of an old hippy from Wolverhampton whom Ray met at Lars resort. Pat had moved to the island to retire and had built a small bungalow up near one of the waterfalls. His Midlands accent reminded Ray of some of his family members back home and, since they were born in the same month within one day of each other, albeit in different years, they got along well. Lily got along well with Pat's Thai wife and they would often socialise together.

Ray and Lily had also become friends with the owners of the local radio station run by a well-to-do Thai couple. Lek was well educated and very beautiful as well as clever. Ray secretly fancied her. Lek's partner Somchai came from a wealthy family on the mainland. She was the main DJ on the radio station, which was the first on the island, and was also a good singer. She was quite the professional entertainer and would MC at various events around the island that were broadcast on the local TV station. They would often enjoy singing karaoke songs with them in their home on top of a mountain next to the radio station.

Then there was Richard from England who had also recently moved to the island. He rented a bungalow near Lars resort. Lars said one day "I have a new neighbour who's a little bit ting tong". When Richard showed up he looked like the spitting image of Johnny Rotten. Lars grinned and said "He's not going to have an easy life here". He was likeable enough, though, and quite genuine, Ray got along with him.

One of the more memorable tourists would also cross their path around that time. Clarence from France was a spiritual man who travelled a lot and had learned about black magic in Indonesia. He was also friends with Pierre in the village. Ray enjoyed chatting with Clarence about the things he had learned on his travels. One day Clarence invited Ray to visit him at his bungalow and to his amazement there were at least a dozen dragonflies hovering over the roof of his home. Clarence had a special energy about him, something similar to the guru Sienna. He wasn't completely honest at first, though. Lily read his palm and told him he had children. At first Clarence denied this but later on, after a few drinks, he came back to tell them that he had a daughter but they didn't get on very well. Lily read many palms and never got it wrong.

Road trips

Business was still going well in the bar even if Ray was no longer enjoying it so much. It was OK in short bursts but he'd seen enough about the game the ladies liked to play with the men who came into the bar. They were skilled in the art of deception and it was all so they could extract money from the men. They were very good at it though and it was best that Ray left them to it because he was too honest which would spoil their games if he talked too much.

He'd spend more time away from the bar and enjoyed going on road trips. Sometimes to the Cambodian border to take a friend for a visa run or sometimes up to Bangkok to drive people to the airport. He'd stay for a couple of nights and catch up with his old friends Vic and Matt who had now moved to the outskirts of Bangkok where Matt was working as an English teacher. Back then teaching English in Thailand was a popular scam if a tourist wanted to stay a bit longer but had run out of money. All it required was a copied university degree which was available from some of the tourist markets and then it was possible to get a job at one of the privately run schools. There were a number of foreigners doing this and Ray met some of Matt's colleagues who were a cheerful bunch. One Xmas they came to stay at his resort.

Ray would also call in to see the Thai couple who used to run the karaoke bar next to his old internet café. They had moved to a smaller place and he'd enjoy a few drinks with them, sometimes going out to play snooker afterwards. On one occasion they played a Thai movie for him to sit and watch with them. It was about a kidnapping of a Bangkok bus and the kidnapper had shot and wounded the driver.

At the end of the film the other passengers didn't turn him into the police even though there was ample opportunity. Instead they forgave him and let him go in the end. It left Ray with a peculiar feeling in his stomach. Of all the other films he'd watching in his life, without exception, if someone had shot and kidnapped people they would get punished by the law or revenged in some way. He'd never seen a film ending quite like it and that night he had to go home early. It later helped him to understand the mind-set of some of the Thai people. Lily later said that's because a lot of the poorer Thais know if they handed him into the police his life would be ruined and they didn't want the karma for that so it's better for them to forgive and let him go.

The road trips were often entertaining and quite trouble free. Occasionally Ray was stopped by the police mainly because he didn't have an international driving license and would have to pay a small fine. Thing is though, in Thailand you can only be fined once a day by the police which made driving somewhat more pleasurable. One time he got caught speeding and paid a small fine. The police turned to him and said he could drive as fast as he liked for the rest of the day. Ray eventually got himself a Thai driving license, quite an easy process given he already had a UK license and no test was required. The Thai license came in rather handy as it meant he could use it as a form of ID and didn't have to pay the extortionate prices charged to foreigners in certain places such as national parks.

The road trips were a welcome distraction from the new atmosphere at the resort. It was still enjoyable and there were some interesting people to chat to but selling sex is a dirty business and the tricks of the trade that the ladies would use were very devious. Ray told them he didn't want them using any black magic. The thing is though, telling a Thai person about rules only gives them an opportunity to manipulate them. It could be off putting too; on one occasion a Russian guy came to him complaining he'd caught an STD from one of the ladies and had later infected his Russian girlfriend. Ray didn't want to know about these things but it was unavoidable given his chosen profession.

That Russian guy turned out to be a good friend though. He had previously worked in the USA as a psychologist and had moved to the island to work as a scuba diving instructor. He knew a lot about drugs and was a contributor to a famous website about drugs. It was through him that Ray got to learn about all the different types of drugs easily available over the counter from a pharmacy in Thailand. Since he owned a pharmacy as part of his resort and had given them a good deal on the rent he was able to get drugs on his doorstep. He didn't get a discount at first, much to his dismay. That required the help of Pierre, the eccentric Frenchman, who introduced him to the pharmacist as his friend. After that he got a discount on anything he bought there.

So Ray did various trips into the world of synthetic drugs. There were some enjoyable trips and it gave him some new insights. One night he was so high on synthetic opium that he was able to speak Thai fluently with a Thai lady who worked as a waitress across the road. He didn't remember much about it but the next day the waitress came to remind him how they sat and had a long conversation in Thai during which Ray got nothing wrong.

He was reminded of something Sienna had taught him. "The spirit knows everything" and "There is no language". Ray supposed that's what he meant by the experience he had that night.

The Fight

Running a brothel meant that Ray would encounter some of the more unsavoury characters on the island. Other people in similar lines of work only a bit more extreme. He'd also meet whoremongers, horny men simply out to get laid.

One man in particular was quite nasty. Tim ran a tailor shop in the same village. He hailed from Nepal and, like many others, had relocated to the island after the tragic tsunami in 2004. The sleepy village that Ray had moved to had turned into a busy place with a lot more businesses opening up.

Anyway Tim had taken a liking to one of Ray's staff. He didn't care much when he called around to see her either which would often be in the middle of the night when he came in to the resort drunk to knock on the door of the bungalow where the ladies were sleeping. Sometimes he'd call round during the day and showed very little respect to anyone else there. He had bloodshot eyes, looked mean and was quite big for an Asian man. Ray didn't feel comfortable about it at all and asked Lily to tell the staff not to let him come over when people were sleeping. Tim didn't pay any attention to this warning so the next time Ray spoke with him directly, explaining he was waking people up when he came in drunk. Tim just sneered at him and paid no attention to what had been said.

This annoyed Ray and one night, after he'd been up late drinking whiskey with some guests, not long after he went to bed heard Tim trying to get into the ladies bungalow again.

Ray was furious and fuelled by the local firewater he'd drank that night, got dressed and went looking for Tim. He marched all the way through the village and back again where he found Tim outside the local convenience store. Ray stormed up to him yelling "STAY OUT OF MY RESORT" and walloped him. It wasn't a punch it was an open handed slap but delivered with full force. Tim fell down stunned. In Ray's drunken haziness and rage he'd temporarily forgotten how Asian men fight – there are no rules. The next moment two of Tim's friends came out of the convenience store and a drunken melee ensued. Ray's was not much of a fighter but managed to defend himself well but still took a few hits. Then at one point two of the men had Ray's arms behind him whilst Tim was about to hit him in the face with a beer bottle. To Ray's amazement Lily appeared from nowhere and dived in front of him screaming "NO, NO, NO". That stunned everyone and Ray and Lily were able to retreat inside their resort.

It didn't stop there though. Back in their room they could hear men's voices in their garden. Ray took a big kitchen knife, stuffed it down the back of his trousers and went to greet them. Lily followed and between them they were able to slowly usher then out of the resort and lock the gate. There was a lot of shouting going on from both sides, obscenities being hurled at each other. The next moment BOOM a beer bottle smashed into the iron grilled gate then a few more. It was Tim who had just returned from the convenience store with some ammunition. Each bottle thrown sounded like a bomb going off. During this chaos Lily was desperately try to contact the police but no one was answering the phone. They hadn't been paying the local police, just as they hadn't in Bangkok because they believed it was the right thing to do, that's why nobody came to help.

Eventually though the police showed up after about an hour and things calmed down. That was the longest hour of their stay on the island.

It had truly been a scary episode. The next day they went to the local police box in the village. Typically the policeman on duty just shrugged his shoulders and didn't want to help. It has been said of the Thai police, when faced with a problem they will look at it and think of two things; 1) Can I get away with doing nothing and 2) What's in it for me.

Luckily for Ray and Lily a good friend of theirs was just passing the police box and came to say hello. Mie was a local DJ on the island and quite an influential figure given his job and large following. In fact his elderly parents were staying at Ray's resort. It meant the police had to take action otherwise they would've been made to look pretty stupid. Saving face means a lot to Thai people. The policeman jumped in his car and rounded up the offenders. Later on he had a chat with Ray and warned him not to go fighting outside his resort. "You should've hit him inside your resort" he laughed. He then surprised Ray with his next comment "We know you're a good guy, you used to work in Holland". Apparently the police have files on all the foreigners living in Thailand.

That fight had certainly stirred things up. Ray felt pretty good about the whole situation because he'd given his devil a bit of fun as he had been taught to do although he was a bit scared about any possible repercussions. Some of the other local expats were a bit offended by the violent behaviour. The local Thais seemed to respect him for it though. After all in Thailand you are allowed to defend your home, in fact if you own a bar over there you are allowed to own a gun too. Ray never went down that road though but he knew other bar owners who had and was offered guns.

One of the Nepalese tailors, who appeared to be the ringleader of the tailors, came to visit Ray one night in his bar to speak about Tim who was his neighbour. "That guy is an idiot", he said. "A few weeks ago he came into my shop and threatened me with a sword. He's jealous because I'm a better salesman than him. If he does it again I will kill him and leave" he said frankly. Judging by the look on his face, Ray took his words seriously.

A few weeks later, whilst Ray was loading up his jeep he looked down the road to see Tim angrily walking towards him with a group of men. Ray looked away and when he looked back again Tim was gone. He never saw him again after that.

The local policeman saw Ray a short while after that at the opening of a new bar complex. He looked over with a knowing smile and said to Ray; "Hey, don't go fighting three men again".

Ray had certainly made an impression on the police.

Events like these gave Ray's soul the experience it was asking for. It certainly was a rollercoaster of emotions but that's what the holographic universe is all about. Whisky will fuel the anger. This was something that Sienna taught about; different types of alcohol gave energy to certain chakras. Whisky fed the will chakra, the one that's 4 fingers below the bellow button; its where our anger sits.

The Lunatics

There were other less desirable people running businesses on the island. One of which was a young thief from England; he was about Ray's age, had never worked a day in his life and sold drugs in his large bar. He was the scourge of most residents in the village because of his irresponsible and rude nature, often playing loud music until 3 or 4am. There was a lot of violence in his bar and his staff cheated a lot of customers. Amazingly, his bar was quite popular though and he often drew a big crowd. That was probably more to do with his Thai wife, who was quite a big lady and had previously worked as a mamasan in other bars. Mia knew her business and took an instant dislike to Ray's wife, Lily, whom she saw as a competitor. Ray wasn't keen on either of them. He tried to get along with the bloke but he was taking so much cocaine and other drugs that he couldn't understand what he was talking about most of the time. The bloke's eyes kept darting all over the place when he was talking, which was most off-putting. They had several run-ins over the years but most of the time they kept away from each other.

Mia, though, seemed to have it in for Lily and had threatened to have her killed serval times.

It was not pleasant to live with. On the island the corrupt police had let this couple flourish simply because they were sharing the profits of their drug dealing with the police. This bothered both Ray and Lily, who made it known to their friends. Lars new them well. "Yeh, he's a little wanker." he said in a matter of fact way.

Then one day one of the mafia kingpins strode in to their bar with some friends. He was only a young, scrawny, Thai man but he was very sure of himself. "If you want our help, your life will change forever." he said in a menacing fashion whilst pointing a bony finger at them. Ray thought about it for a while and then politely declined the offer. They drank a few beers, played some pool and left, never to return.

Boy, was he glad he turned them down. Ray would go on to meet foreigners who had said "Yes" in the heat of the moment to the offer of help from the mafia. They then became part of their family and that's not a nice situation to be in. The mafia could show up with their group of friends at their business whenever they felt like it and help themselves to what they wanted. They'd also use some people to do jobs for them. Ray was so relieved he turned them down.

The best road trip

The road trip to Laos was one to remember. Ray and Lily left some friends in charge of their resort, Raymond from Holland and his Thai partner Pooky.

Raymond worked as a professional football coach. He clearly enjoyed his life and had studied with such Dutch greats as Marco Van Basten and Ruud Gullit. He was a customer of the internet cafe and they had remained friends. Pooky in particular was thrilled to be running a resort for a couple of weeks – living out her dream.

They stopped in Bangkok at their luxury condo and enjoyed a couple of nights out there before heading up to Lily's home town to celebrate her daughter's birthday. It was around March time, which is the start of the main school holiday.

In the hometown Ray asked one of the cousins to buy some ganja so they could all enjoy a smoke. They made a home-made bong out of a plastic water bottle and bamboo shoots – this was typically Thai.

They were sitting in a room with a small group of Thai people, about 7 or 8. One of the Thai guys took the first puff of the bong, looked directly at Ray as he exhaled and immediately burst out laughing hysterically. Ray couldn't fathom out whether it was simply the effect of the ganja or if the Thai man was laughing at him. As soon as Ray took a puff, it didn't really matter anymore.

They took Lily's daughter and a couple of her friends with them on the road to Laos where Ray would renew his visa.

Laos is a poorer country that borders Thailand to the north. A lot of the poorer farmer families from the north east of Thailand originate from Laos. Since Lily had never been there, it was to be an adventurous trip.

It's a long journey by road to the Laos border and they stopped for one night at a hotel in a town midway on their journey.

Everything is so accessible in Thailand. Food, accommodation or things to do are all affordable and easy to find. So they checked into a mid-range hotel which cost less than 10 pounds for the night per room and enjoyed a night out in that town – a nice meal and a few drinks then back to the clean air-conditioned hotel room.

Ray was eager to hit the road early because his visa was due to expire that day and he needed to cross the border. He wanted to take the car over the border but hadn't managed to get the necessary visa from the Laos embassy in Bangkok. So they left the car in a parking lot close to the Thai/Laos friendship bridge and went over by foot.

As always, dotted along the no-mans land between Thailand and its bordering countries there were casinos and duty free shops. These casinos were always full of gambling mad Thais, who would show up in minibuses daily. Ray would enjoy playing the fruit machines and always put a 10 pounds limit on what he would spend. It was a nice way to while away an hour or two, depending on how lucky he was.

Quite often Thai people would come to speak with him, telling how much they had lost or won, well mostly lost. Interestingly, Ray learned that all of those border casinos were owned by Thai people. Some had a hotel in the same building – a nice 4 star hotel too that only cost 10 pounds for a night.

In Laos Lily was fascinated to be in the country of her ancestors. The food was almost double the price of food in Thailand. They later learned that this is because Laos is not so developed. There is not so much farming going on, making the food more expensive; some of it was imported from Thailand. They spent the night in a nice guest house on the waterfront looking over the Mekhong river in the Laos capital Vientiane. Ray had some of his favourite beer Laos. They had a dark and light beer, both were exquisite and cheap at around 30 pence for a big litre bottle.

The visa renewal was a formality and they crossed back over the border. There they picked up the car and drove to a northern city, to catch up with one of Lily's best friends. Her friend had married a politician from that city and they dropped in to see them on their way home. They had a very grand house that was built in the shape of a giant cube with huge, thick, solid teak doors on every side that could be opened up, concertina style, revealing the luxury furnishings throughout. The property had a large driveway, with luxury cars parked outside the house and with its own fishing lake.

It was a truly stunning home but more was to come in the shape of the Thai politician and the stories he had to tell.

Tod was the number 2 politician in that town and, as he put it, was the one who did all the work. "The number 1 politician just looks good and talks to the media," he laughed. Lily was nattering away with her best friend whilst Ray was admiring the view and playing with the 2 large golden retrievers. Lily told him that her friend had recently had a big row with her husband and in her rage drove to Bangkok and bought the luxury people carrier that was one of the cars parked outside. Ray just smiled and glanced over at her friend who was also smiling yet who didn't show any signs of being ashamed at buying a 30 thousand pound car because she was in a bad mood.

That home was just dripping with money. The furnishings inside were overwhelming in their luxuriousness. The best wooden cabinets that had been hand made to fit, as well as the best silk curtains.

Later on they had a few drinks. Tod showed them his wine collection, telling them one bottle was worth 20 thousand pounds. Then he started to open another saying it was worth 400 pounds. It was a very nice drop indeed and Ray started telling Tod about his love of beer Laos but that he was disappointed that he wasn't able to bring any across the border. The Thais are very proud people and tend to support their own beers and one imagines they must find it a bit embarrassing that one of their poorer neighbours has a far superior beer. Tod picked up his phone and called a friend. Within an hour a pickup truck delivered 4 crates of beer Laos; 2 each of the dark and light beers. Ray was impressed and enjoyed drinking some of his favourite Asian beer; understandably, Tod stuck with Thai beer.

Tod regaled them all with some tales of his duties as the number 2 man in town. Once he had to stop an aeroplane from taking off, at the request of the local police because there was a wanted fugitive on board.

It certainly was impressive to drink with a man who was in a position of power. Even more so that Ray had ended up a guest in his home; he felt honoured.

"Stay as long as you like." Tod said cheerfully. They stayed a few days, enjoying the luxury surroundings with the sun beating down, the golden retrievers to play with, fresh fish from the lake and good beer to drink. Tim was a busy man and would be out most of the time. Sometimes he would have meetings at home. All sorts of high- level people would show up; at one time some representatives from Forbes came to the house.

Ray and Lily needed to leave, to get back to the guest house, and they still had some other friends to visit on the way home. Tod asked them to stay longer but they politely declined because they had to go.

Thais have an expression called "Gring Jai", which means they feel a bit guilty at putting someone else out. Ray and Lily also felt this way because Tod had made them feel very welcome and given them a lot.

There was one last parting gift that was given to them by Tod which Ray would learn about when they got back to the resort.

Next stop on the road home was to see Denis and wife, their friends from the island who used to run a resort there. Denis had paid to have a nice new house for his wife's family and they went to christen it with beer Laos and some other goodies bought from the Laos duty free shop, red wine and a bottle of Jack Daniels silver label.

They were all big drinkers. It was the reason why they went into the hospitality business in Thailand.

Denis had been working back in Denmark since he left the island in order to save money. It was his plan to arrange for his wife to go over there to stay with him.

That afternoon they met a shaman whilst drinking in their friends' garden. He was a 50 year old man but looked to be in his mid 30's. He never went to school; instead he spent most of his life as a monk. When he left the temple he spent some time in the jungle doing meditation and he learned – as he put it, 'by listening to plants' - how to make herbal medicine.

A very intuitive man, he could see right through Ray and Lily, describing their personalities and relationship - he got it spot on. Also drinking with them that day was a Denis' mother inlaw who was

66. She had just recovered from cancer. When she was first diagnosed with cancer she went to the local hospital to get chemotherapy. She became very thin and her hair fell out. Then she decided to try the herbal medicine from the shaman and after a while was cured. That day they saw her hair had grown back and she looked very strong for her age.

The next day they went to the Shaman's home. It was a modest two up two down house. In his lounge were barrels of herbs, dried flowers and leaves. He showed them his files of all the people he had treated. They saw photos of their friends' mum before and after treatment. Also people who had had serious traffic accidents and could not walk, were able to walk again, although some needed a walking stick.

He then performed a quick health check on Ray and Lily. Ray had to stretch his arm out and he held it whilst pinching something close to his armpit. His left arm went numb - this is a good sign apparently - but his right arm did not. Ray told him of the operation he had to repair damaged shoulder ligaments and the shaman warned him he could lose feeling in his right arm when he got older.

Ray took 3 bottles of his medicine to give it a try. He said it cured a number of illnesses.

The Gift

Back at the resort Lily and Ray discovered what the gift from the powerful politician was.

One day the tourist police pulled up outside their resort and came in for a chat. They were setting up camp on the island and needed a place to stay. They had also heard about the death threats from their nasty neighbours and wanted to help. They seemed like a friendly bunch and Ray gave them a room in the resort to use whilst they were waiting for their accommodation to be built.

This was the start of another adventure into the world of the tourist police. These guys have a position of power in Thailand.

A number of them had second wives and were involved in other businesses.

The senior sergeant major was quite friendly and would often go out drinking with them. In fact they were out late one night, about 5am, and Ray wanted to go home because they were due to go out on a boat trip at 6am. "Don't worry, I have to start work soon too" laughed the senior sergeant major. He was a jovial character and looked out for them. One time their motorbike had a puncture whilst driving over one of the mountain and he came to pick them up in his police car. He'd often promise to give Ray some help in renewing his visa, because he had some friends working in immigration on the nearby border crossing.

They were proving to be useful allies and made them feel somewhat safer. It hadn't been enjoyable living with death threats, especially when you consider bar owners are allowed to own guns.

One night they were invited to a police party at a large resort in another village. It was run by a Frenchman and his Thai wife. Frank was also a musician and played in a band on the island. There they met many police officers and even met some who worked as undercover police. One of them was dressed up in a police uniform, sat at their table all night chatting with the other police. Later on, Lily told Ray they had discovered he was not even a policeman. As the evening went on a call came through to say there was a gunfight in a village on the other side of the island between some angry Thais. Ray thought that would be the end of the party but the police stayed put, saying they didn't want to get involved in a gun fight.

It was a vivid insight into their mind-set. They would often tell stories about deaths on the island. Mainly, these were from accidents such as people drowning in the sea.

One evening one of the tourist police invited Ray and Lily into his room to meet his second wife. She was a drug dealer and they tried some yabbah for the first time. This at the time was a popular speed-like drug in Thailand. Later on the police gave Ray his gun to hold, fully loaded. Ray was once again amazed at how open and friendly they were, not to mention the shock value they provided.

The Tree House

Since Ray was still a bit fed up with the brothel being run in the bar, Lily arranged for her family to construct a raised hut in their garden as a sort of retreat to be used to escape the chaos.

The younger brother, Bah, and his friends were given a chance to redeem themselves after the disaster at the internet café. They did a pretty good job, too, in constructing a very sturdy raised hut with guidance from Lily's father. There were no steps, though; so for a while Ray had to climb a Thai style ladder, which is a plank of wood criss-crossed with smaller pieces of wood. It was a bit of fun that grew tiresome after a while and in the end one of Lar's brother in- laws constructed some proper steps.

To put the finishing touches to it, the father in-law sent his alcoholic son, the one who looked like Gollum, to do the painting and varnishing. It worked out well for both of them; the father got a break from his alcoholic son and Gollum got to stay in the resort - which he enjoyed immensely. He took full advantage of the situation, too, dragging out his work to last several months.

It was not easy sometimes; Gollum being an alcoholic would sometimes wake up guests early in the morning, begging for money because he needed some booze. Ray had a couple of arguments with him and it was through this experience that he learned how seriously Thais take their culture when it comes to respect.

Gollum was older than them and therefore had to be respected. "Yeh, but he can't go around waking up our guests." Ray would fume to Lily, who seemed reluctant to do anything about it.

Even the times when the father in-law stayed were awkward. He was quite elderly and suffered from arthritis. When they were busy in the resort he stayed in the bungalow which had a bunk-bed. If the son was sleeping there, too, the father insisted on sleeping in the higher bunk. Because he was older he had to be higher, making the difficult climb up the ladder to the top bunk each night. That was a very strict rule in their society, but they were able to laugh about it.

Ray spoke with Pierre about this and Pierre told him that the main things his sons learnt at school were "Respect, respect and respect".

That's how it was over there. It was a "being" society. Gurdjieff wrote about this, how people are made up of two main things; knowledge and being. The Thais were most definitely more focussed on the being side of life.

Upon completion of the raised hut, Ray now had what would become his favourite room in the resort. There was enough room for a sofa, some chairs and a table. He would often enjoy playing chess with friends or smoking a joint with a beer. It really was idyllic. Gollum had done a fantastic job of varnishing and painting the place.

Around that time they had a new regular guest in the form of Stan from Dublin. He was a huge man with an amazing intellect. Stan had several university degrees, including a PhD from the London school of Economics. He had been working as a university teacher at a university in Vietnam for a few years and had some amazing stories to tell. Whenever he came, people learnt something new. His mind was full of knowledge and he loved to share it.

The downward spiral

Even though he'd met plenty of interesting people and had enjoyed many good days and nights on the island, things were taking their toll and Ray was starting to get restless. In the bar one night Ray got very drunk on whisky and ended up having sex with one of the ladies in the toilet. Lily found out about it and was furious for a long time. To be clear, many Thais understood about human nature and it was accepted for someone in a relationship to be unfaithful, so long as wasn't seen by their partner. Ray had committed a fatal mistake in getting caught and this was the beginning of the end of his relationship with Lily. Lily found it very hard to forgive him for his moment of madness, because she lost face.

Another of Lily's brothers and his wife came to stay with them at the resort and sold Thai food. It came as a welcome distraction. The ladies working in the bar left, to make way for a more family orientated resort. There was a nicer atmosphere and business was good. It was short lived because the brother in-law and his wife, who seemed to be enjoying the riches for the first time in their lives, fell out over money. It was on the cards. Ray would watch the wife greedily counting money at the end of the day. It was a lot of money, too, and they expanded their business by investing in motorcycles to rent out. They split up, though, and the wife moved to another beach on the island to open a small restaurant. She wasn't prosperous there, though, and Ray wondered why she didn't simply go back home. "She can't." Lily explained. "Last time she was in the village she was showing off to everyone about how rich she had become and telling them all to follow her. If she goes back it will be loss of face".

Still, they had provided some pleasant memories. One night they hosted a birthday party for one of their friends at the resort and a lot of people came. There was dancing in the bar; in the garden people sat and talked and in the tree house people smoked joints. It was a very good atmosphere and there were lots of smiling faces.

Then one day the father in-law and brother in-law had an accident in their pickup truck on the island. Ray and Lily showed up shortly after it happened. It clearly wasn't their fault, as the skid marks on the road indicated that the oncoming vehicle had lost control because it was going too fast; this was backed up by the brother in-law's story. The police were on the side of the other young driver, though. They gave Ray a smug grin as he walked past. That was another lesson in Thai culture; it's all about who you know. Even though they were in the wrong, they got away with it because the driver had better connections.

Around that time Ray's resort was robbed. He'd gotten drunk on whisky and ran his mouth off about some of the expats he didn't get along with. They got their revenge by stealing some money and some of Lily's Jewellery.

Then the monk from Lily's hometown died. They had visited him not long before and he smiled at Ray saying "You look dark.", which reflected Ray's mood entirely. The monk looked dark too and died of leukaemia shortly afterwards. He had a lot of love for people and had been to Ray's wedding and had stayed at his resort to bless it.

His body was kept in a glass coffin for 1 year after his death so that people could pay their respects. This was common in Thailand for their revered monks. On the day Ray and Lily went to the temple to pay their respects, they sat on the floor with a small crowd of Thais, with the coffin at the end of the room. As he sat there looking at the monk's body, it appeared to Ray as if the monk's head turned to look in their direction; not physically, it was more of a silhouette of his head that turned. Ray immediately thought he was seeing things, but when they left the temple Lily turned to him and asked if he saw the monk's head move. Then a few more Thais said they saw it too.

This confirmed something else that Sienna once spoke about. He said that when the physical body dies, the emotional and intellectual bodies live on. Monks are working on their emotional bodies and in the case of this monk he must have developed his emotional body to the point where he had some control of it, even after his physical body died.

The final nail in the coffin came in the form of another guest from Germany, Michael. He was a nice enough man, although very fragile. He was a musician and very sensitive. Ray got along well with him and learned that Michael had a pacemaker and had died four times in his life. This interested Ray, as Michael told him about his experiences with death and how he saw a tunnel with a bright light at the end of it on each occasion. "Don't worry, I won't die in your resort." Michael laughed. A few weeks later, at around 4am, there was a frantic knocking on Ray's door. "HE'S DEAD, HE'S DEAD" Michael's girlfriend for the night was screaming. Ray anxiously went to Michael's room to find him collapsed on the bed with no signs of life. Ray listened and felt for a pulse and there was none, Michael had stopped breathing. Ray then gave him a few gentle slaps on the face, whilst calling his name; but still the body lay lifeless. Ray sat on the end of the bed worrying and wondering what to do next. Then all of a sudden Michael leapt up with his eyes wide open as if he'd received an electric shock. He was a bit stunned but soon calmed down. Ray bought some food for him and they chatted for a while in the garden. Even though the whole experience was frightening, Ray managed to raise a laugh by saying "Hey, you promised you wouldn't die in my resort.".

Ray was disheartened and took all these events as a signal that he should move on. A few days later, he drank some home-made rice whisky and went berserk in his bar throwing a bottle into the ceiling and shouting his head off. For several weeks after that he was passing blood whenever he went to the toilet. This scared the life out of Ray and he took it to mean he should stop drinking. In fact, stop with the bar business altogether. He'd had enough of it.

The Fishing Park Adventure.

Their friends at the Radio station, Lek and Somchai, suggested they take a look at a fishing park they were interested in selling on the mainland. If they liked it, they could move there and Lek would help them to sell their resort.

Lek and Somchai took them to their fishing park and it blew them away. It truly was a stunning home. It was a huge place with a large house, restaurant, karaoke room and a massive fishing lake with a walkway to raised huts in the water and a small island at the end. It really looked like heaven on earth and it was peaceful, too, set in a quiet village near the coast and not too far from a big city. Ray and Lily both fell in love with the place immediately. Ray was a bit concerned about the location, being close to the coast and on low lying land. Somchai assured them that there was no problem with flooding; he had built the place himself and never had a problem with flooding. Ray and Lily decided they wanted to move in. They had known Lek and Somchai for several years and had socialised with them often. Somchai had been a monk before and they had no reason to doubt him.

Somchai's mother was looking after the place whilst they had moved to the island to open the radio station. She showed the ownership papers, which looked legitimate, to Ray and Lily. She took a shine to Ray for some reason. Lek was keen to get a deposit out of Ray as a down payment for the property. They agreed on 4 thousand pounds, which would cover one year's stay at the fishing park. If they decided to buy it within the first year, it would cost 6 million baht and, after the one year was up, it would cost 7 million baht. Ray's resort was valued at 10 million so he felt pretty good about the whole scenario because, if he did choose to sell it and move there, he would have some cash left over to develop the place. They were thinking of building some bungalows around the lake to rent out to friends.

In exchange Lek would look after their resort and help them to sell it, assuring them she knew plenty of rich people.

Lek did most of the talking because she was good at it and could speak English well. Somchai remained pretty quiet most of the time.

They hired a truck and moved all their belongings to the fishing park. Lily's brother came with them too.

A few expat friends had warned Ray not to do business with Thai people but Ray needed to press ahead with this adventure. His heart told him it was the right thing to do.

Lek was being increasingly nice to Ray and would often call him and flirt over the phone. He felt quite thrilled that such a powerful, clever, beautiful lady gave him so much attention.

On the day he handed over 1000 pounds of the deposit Lek was clearly ecstatic that she had some money. Ray felt good too, moving to a dream home and no longer had the chaos of life running a resort on the holiday island. He looked up at the sky that night and saw the clouds looked like a huge galleon passing. He took this to mean his boat had come in. Somchai and Lek were busy thinking up more ways to extract money from Ray.

Somchai took Lily to a finance company in the city and tried to get her to take out a loan against their jeep. It wasn't possible, though, because they hadn't finished paying the loan on the jeep.

They were still demanding more money from Ray, though, and he thought to ask his friend Pat on the island about it. Pat had just inherited some money from his Mum.

Lek drove Ray to the island. He was quite thrilled to be alone with her and she used her manipulative skills to the fullest. She smiled at him and said "You need to know how to do business in Thailand." Ray was tempted to jump into bed with her but after all the upsets he had been through, and knowing how people loved to gossip on the island, he decided it best not to put Lily though any more suffering.

He duly borrowed the money from Pat and was able to pay the full deposit to Lek. In exchange she would pay some rent on his resort, only a small amount, whilst she tried to sell it for him. Ray wasn't too concerned; they had an income coming from the condominium which at that time had been rented to a Russian rally driver. They had enough to live and it shouldn't be long until they could sell the resort.

The cracks were starting to appear. Lek and Somchais' true motives were becoming clear. Shortly after that, there was a big storm on the island and it washed away their radio station. The repair work cost the same amount they had taken from Ray. It was instant karma at its best. Yet still they carried on with their deceptive game.

Ray knew what was going on but wasn't too concerned. He had a nice quiet home and spent time feeding the fish, walking the dogs around the lake and meditating on the island. Life was blissful there. Lily was happy working with her brother, taking care of the huge gardens. Ray was still infatuated with Lek and one afternoon, during one of his walks around the lake, he looked into the water and in the reflection could see a perfect ring around the sun. He'd never seen anything like that before and took it to be part of the magical feeling he had inside his heart whenever he thought about Lek.

Lily was furious with what was going on. "Did you have sex with her on the island ?" she seethed. "Some Thai men use their wives like that to make money for them. She's been slicing away at you since the day you first met.". She was right but Ray wasn't really interested; he was enjoying the nice feeling in his heart.

Lek and Somchai would take them out to nice restaurants and karaoke bars. However Lek got quite concerned when he learned that Ray and Lily had made friends with some of the locals in the village. He obviously had something to hide and didn't socialise with them after that.

Instead he would work on renovating old cars which he did at the fishing park, using his high powered tools which contributed towards a high electricity bill. He didn't offer to pay anything towards it. Ray knew he was being ripped off but just couldn't understand what he hoped to gain from acting like that.

Lek had stopped calling Ray. He wondered why so and went to the resort to investigate. It was closed and looked dirty and run down. Peering through the bar window, he could see a large set of speakers. It looked like they had a big party there. He phoned Lek but again no answer.

Shortly after that, Ray made his annual trip back to England to see his family and renew his visa. Upon his return Lily told him that, whilst he was away, there was a lot of rain and the entire place had flooded badly. It was another deception from Somchai. They'd lost a lot of baby fish they were breeding in a small lake, they were not happy.

Lek phoned Ray asking for more money. She was under the impression he would bring more money with him back from England.

Somchai then made it very clear that they were no longer welcome at the fishing park by leaving his collection of bullets on their bed one afternoon.

Ray and Lily were fed up by this point and drove to the island to speak with Lek. She apologised for not paying any rent, blaming it on the Thai government and handed over the keys to the resort. Their arrogance was quite astounding at times.

Back at the resort Ray and Lily were shocked to find that a lot of their equipment was missing. In total they calculated it was over a thousand pounds worth of kit that was needed to run the resort – electric shower, fan, pool cues and other items had vanished.

Lek and Somchai denied any wrong-doing. None of the bills had been paid and the modem was missing too. Something was very wrong. One of their neighbours said that they saw Lek and Somchai fill up three pickup trucks with their belongings.

Ray was certainly naïve to trust them so easily. He'd only just realised that they had been at war with him the entire time.

He was still obsessed with Lek, though. He couldn't get her out of his mind and even had dreams about her. They were very real and vivid dreams too. Ray had some sort of energetic effect on electrical devices too. Whatever he seemed to touch, even if it was turning on a light switch, it buzzed with energy and broke. "She's done black magic on you." Lily said furiously. Ray didn't know what was going on.

Lily was fed up and left to visit her hometown, leaving Ray alone at the resort.

He was confused and fed up. After all, he'd just survived a war in trying to do business with Thai people and he was back at the resort on the island, a place he'd been keen to leave before.

He sold the pool table to raise some much needed cash and then advertised the resort for rent. Luckily, he struck up some deals quickly, renting the rooms to an Indian neighbour and the bar to a Frenchman. Around the same time the Russian tenant at the condo handed in his notice; this worked out well because they could go and live there.

They'd never spent much time at the condo but now they had a rental income from the resort. Things were frosty between Ray and Lily, though, and they were arguing a lot every day. They were still in shock from what had happened at the fishing park and he still couldn't get Lek out of his head. He kept phoning her and sending messages to no avail.

Lily took a job in Bangkok working for a health food company and Ray spent his days doing what he was best at, taking it easy.

A few weeks went by and one day Lily received a phone call from a Thai man claiming to be the owner of the fishing park saying Somchai had sold it to him 3 years ago.

They drove to the fishing park and, sure enough, he showed them the up-to-date land papers with his signature on it. The papers Somchai's mum had shown them were out of date. Even that sweet old Thai lady was in on the scam.

That night they had a drink with some of the neighbours in the village who had some interesting stories to tell. One neighbour said that Somchai had tried to steal land from him by moving the land posts late at night. When Ray asked how much land he'd lost the neighbour said "It was big enough to bury him in.". They fell about laughing at that comment. Apparently Somchai had performed the same scam on several other people at the fishing park. He really did turn out to be a bad apple. Lek was not so sweet and innocent either. There were lots of stories about her sleeping around with high ranking officials to gain favours. A while later Somchai's sister showed up and joined in the fun. She too was a DJ and had previously worked with Lek. At one point she asked Ray "Did you dream about Lek?", looking concerned as if she knew this had happened to other people. Ray was stunned as he thought to himself "How the hell can someone get into your dream?"

The next day Somchai showed up at the fishing park and promptly kicked them out. Since they'd had only 6 months there, Ray asked for half the money back. Of course he didn't get it.

They returned to Bangkok and went to see their old friend, Bard, the police colonel. He told Ray; "Thai people are very bad when doing business. There is no win-win situation, only a winner and loser". He checked up on Lek and Somchai and said they were part of a criminal group.

Lily wouldn't let go of the situation and wanted to fight them some more. Somchai threatened her with videos he'd made of them sleeping in the fishing park. Apparently there was a hidden camera in the bedroom and bathroom. It was such an elaborate scam that took them years to pull off and, during that time, they had befriended them for several years in advance. Ray admired their skills of deception.

Apparently Somchai died a few months later in a fishing accident.

The Nun.

Ray was now broken, confused and exhausted. At least he had a comfy home in Bangkok to chill out in. Things were not going well with Lily, as they were still arguing a lot. He thought of going back to England to start a new life but didn't relish that thought at all.

He was still infatuated with Lek and tried to get her attention online. Ray was using the internet a lot at home and had developed some skills in web design. He knew of websites to advertise on and would place messages in the lonely hearts column to attract Lek. She answered once, although it wasn't a nice message, something to do with having a rotten life.

Ray was still undeterred, though; he was obsessed with her. The fact that she'd taken him to such emotional highs and lows made him want more.

That's when he wrote an ad in the lonely hearts column with words to the effect of:

"Looking for a beautiful, intelligent woman to take me up on emotional highs and then drop me like a stone."

Yes, he really wrote that, but at the time it seemed like the right thing to do. A few days later he got an answer. It wasn't from Lek though, but another beautiful Thai lady called Sandra who worked in an office just down the road from Ray's condo. In Ray's mind this was all meant to be and was in fitting with his adventure in the holographic universe.

Ray met with Sandra at a coffee shop on the ground floor of a plush looking office block. She was of average height and build, very attractive and clever – working as the communications director for a big company. She was single and had no children, a career woman.

"Did you mean what you wrote in the ad?" Sandra laughed. "Of course not", smiled Ray. "Oh you should be careful what you wish for." she said with a glint in her eye. They got along well and had a similar sense of humour. They sat and chatted for half an hour or so before Sandra had to return to work.

Ray went home and logged onto MSN where he chatted with Sandra for hours. They laughed a lot and Sandra admitted to him "Ray, I really like you a lot.". What was it about Ray and Thai ladies? He was fascinated with them and they seemed to love him. Ray felt great.

They would chat every day and meet at the local coffee shop for a few weeks. Sandra came from a wealthy Thai family and had been raised in America. She spoke English with an American accent yet looked Thai.

Ray told Sandra all about his mission to give everything up and get it back fifty times. She listened intently and seemed genuinely concerned. Ray was on a high, he felt completely comfortable with Sandra and it was as if he'd found salvation.

"I have a well-connected family and may be able to help you" Sandra enthused. Ray felt as if everything was falling into place. Then she stunned Ray by saying "The Nun said it's my duty to help you complete your mission.".

"Who's the Nun?" Ray asked perplexed.

"She's a revered, elderly, lady monk who has reached enlightenment and can see the past, present and future. I'm one of her disciples.".

Ray was feeling over the moon, like all his Christmases had come at once. He felt all tingly inside because this appealed to his imaginative and spiritual nature.

And one man saved humanity.

They received an emergency call from the bar and had to go to the island because the Frenchman who was renting their bar had fallen out with his Thai partner. They wanted out and needed help.

It was easily solved because the bar was in a good location; another tenant was found and a contract signed.

Then they met up with one of their old guests from Switzerland, Jean-Paul. He was an interesting character they first met on his around the world trip when he stayed in their resort and watched every episode of Seinfeld in order to improve his English. He looked ugly and clumsy but was in fact very clever and worked as the financial controller for one of the Swiss watch companies. He was a big drinker, too, one of the best in their bar. He'd returned to Thailand for a holiday and went with Lily and Ray in their jeep back to Bangkok.

Along the way they stopped at another island to visit their old friends, Paul and Tao. Paul was the old rocker who had studied with a guru in India.

Ray and Lily were still arguing a lot. She loved to dig up the past, and, when they checked into the hotel on the island, Lily stayed in the room whilst Ray went out with Jean-Paul for a few drinks.

First stop was a bar on the beach where they played pool with some local Thai guys. The losers had to jog around the table once. During the games Ray couldn't help but notice a luxury yacht in the bay. The sun had gone down and it was hard to see clearly, but there was someone on deck with an infrared camera pointing in their direction. Ray felt suspicious but thought nothing more of it.

The next bar was a Thai Coyote bar in the main village. To be clear, a Coyote bar is aimed at Thais and other Asians. They have beautiful hostesses who dance and will sit with customers if you buy them a drink. You must understand the local customs and, since Ray had been there for several years, he was welcome there and felt comfortable. Jean-Paul bought a lot of drinks for the ladies and they enjoyed their company in the small bar. Then all of a sudden, the stereo in the bar stopped playing Thai music and on came and there was an English voice yelling enthusiastically "And one man saved humanity.", followed by a crowd of people cheering "Ray, Ray, Ray" over and over. Ray's heart skipped a beat and his next thought was it's a hallucination. Then Jean-Paul tapped him on the shoulder saying; "Hey, they're singing about you" and then carried on drinking with the ladies. It couldn't be a hallucination, if Jean-Paul heard it too.

Ray was flummoxed, scared too and yet absolutely thrilled at the same time. Was it really true that he was involved in something that was going to save humanity? That's a tall order and a scary proposition. It is what the holographic universe is about, though, and it was what he had studied for and indeed his purpose in giving everything up. That's a huge weight to carry, a lot of responsibility.

The next day he went to an internet café and looked up online to see if there were any such music tracks that he'd heard in the bar that night. He couldn't find anything. Then he saw that Sandra was online and had a chat with her, telling her what he'd been up to after leaving Bangkok abruptly. It was good to talk with her and he felt great; his heart felt full and his life had meaning and purpose.

Later that day he had a chat with his friend Paul and told him about his new friend in Bangkok. He felt as if he was on the crest of a wave.

The "Sale"

Back in Bangkok Ray expressed his concerns to Sandra about the nun. He'd only heard about her and wanted to see her. Sandra got really mad; "She won't see you, she's too busy and in any case, if you meet her, what are you going to do?" Ray could see her point but still had some doubts. Sandra left work early that day and drove Ray to a temple on the outskirts of Bangkok to meet with another disciple of the nun. He was an elderly Thai man who lived in a house that had no electricity. He gave Ray a filthy look when he arrived and kept his distance during the entire meeting.

"Did you see the way he treated you?" Sandra asked on the journey home. "You're covered in black magic; that's why he didn't want to be near you". Ray felt terrible. "Lily has been feeding you the dried blood from her menstruation; that's one of the ways they control their men with black magic". Ray was shocked and didn't know what to say. It made him more determined, though; he now took this trip into the holographic universe very seriously. The next day Sandra phoned and sounded very concerned. "The nun has just called me and said there is someone in your family who is very sick. It's a close family member and someone who is overweight". Ray knew that this could only be his father or brother. "What do I need to do?" he asked worriedly. "You need to get them a coffin by way of a blessing". Ray looked around his condo, it wasn't that big and a coffin would certainly fill the room up. "There isn't enough room for a coffin here" Sandra burst out laughing and, when she calmed down eventually, said "No, silly, the coffin stays in the temple with the nun. All you need to do is pay for it and I will transfer the money to the nun." Each coffin cost 100 pounds. He bought two because he wasn't sure if it was his Dad or his brother and duly transferred the money to Sandra who took care of the rest.

Blessings using a coffin are quite common in Buddhist Thailand and Ray felt relieved that he'd helped his family. He bought a coffin for each of his family members and friends.

The next day Sandra phoned Ray again sounding anxious as she explained that one of his cousins was over-weight and drinking too much and was close to death. Ray knew which one it was. If it wasn't for her he wouldn't have come to Thailand. He loved her a lot and wanted to help. "The nun says that in order to save her life you must save someone else's life first". Ray didn't know what to do but Sandra phoned around a few hospitals and found someone who needed an urgent transplant that required a donation. Ray sent the money off for that, over 1,000 pounds. He also called his Auntie to warn her what was going on with her daughter. She'd been concerned about her drinking in the past and the fact that a psychic monk had said she is close to death warranted a phone call, Ray thought. After all his Auntie had developed psychic powers too. He had hoped that she would contribute some money towards the donation but she didn't. Since Ray was running low on funds he sold his car.

Ray firmly believed in Sandra and the nun who seemed to know him and his family better than he did. Even though their methods seemed strange, Ray recalled his teachings with Sienna. "The whole world is used to thinking in a linear way, but we are more than that; there is the circular way too". Ray figured this is what the nun was using; circular thinking, and she had such a wise view of the universe that she could tell in which direction to act. It all seemed so real and Ray was feeling ecstatic.

The next time Ray spoke with Sandra she told him more about the black magic his wife had been doing to him. "She's been feeding you the dried blood from her menstruation". Ray felt alarmed yet disgusted and another chill went down his spine. This had become an all too familiar feeling. "A lot of poorer Thai ladies do this to their men because they believe it will control them." Sandra continued in a matter of fact way, as if it were normal behaviour. Ray felt stiff with fear as Sandra spoke, "Generally they use hair cuttings, toenail clippings or photos to perform the black magic; those are the most common methods."

"All this time you've she's been tricking you, Ray, manipulating you so that she can screw around and enjoy herself. You're the laughing stock of the island, Ray, because all the Thais know what Lily is doing behind your back. Her daughter is working as a prostitute, too, and her father has been supporting her financially". Ray felt saddened and annoyed. He'd been led to believe that Lily's ex-husband didn't support his daughter so Ray had taken on that responsibility. He was distraught to find out that he'd been deceived all this time.

The next day Sandra phoned and sounded concerned. "Are you feeling OK?", she said. Ray felt fine and asked why she had phoned. "The nun had been on the phone to say Lily has been doing more black magic with you" she said frantically. "The black magic she's done is to make you feel sick, to hurt your lungs.". Ray was starting to feel all queasy. "Is there a way I can stop it?" he asked. "The nun doesn't know how it's been done and we're not sure". Ray wasn't certain if he would be affected or even if his wife would do such a thing. Over the next few days a huge rash developed over his chest. Was it black magic or simply because he'd believed in what Sandra was telling him? He was in a state of total panic. Sandra phoned back with a cure "We've found out it's in her knitting! Lily was an avid knitter, often making beer mats and other items out of wool. "You must find her knitting needles, bend them and then unravel all that she has made recently which, funnily enough, was a very tight fitting woollen jumper". Ray did all of that, stealing her knitting when she wasn't looking. "Now put it all in a bag and place it under a tree". Ray duly obliged and the rash soon disappeared. He'd never been sick like that before.

"You must reverse all the black magic she's been doing to you and take everything back from her." Sandra said. Ray was understandably very keen to do so and asked how it could be done.

"All the money you have given to support Lily's daughter must be put into goodwill.". Ray tried to work out roughly how much he'd given over the years. He came to an approximate figure; before he spoke it, Sandra said the same amount, which worked out to be thousands of pounds.

"The nun says you need to raise that money and put it into goodwill before the Thai New Year." Ray urgently set about borrowing money from whoever he could. Sending emails to everyone in his address book asking for money. He phoned family members and friends too. He raised the money, too, and was quite amazed at the feat. He'd not asked for financial help from his family before and was surprised by their generosity. Even Sienna helped, arranging through his family to send him some money.

The money was wired over to him and he had to pick it up from the bank in the middle of the Thai New Year celebrations. Luckily some banks were open and the nearest one was at a shopping mall about a mile down the road. No taxis were available, so he had to walk. Thai New Year is a water festival and Ray had experienced plenty of them; in fact he'd grown a bit weary of them. He got absolutely soaked walking to the bank, arriving there drenched. With squelching shoes he picked up the money and transferred it to Sandra. It still wasn't quite enough, though, so he stole some jewellery from his wife and sold that to raise the extra cash. He was so relieved to get it done on time.

After the New Year Sandra called to say he had to take back the property he'd bought for Lily. "That's why you didn't get it back 50 times, because you didn't give it in a good way.".

That's when Sandra introduced Ray to her father. George was an older Thai man, quite short yet well built. He too had lived in America for 30 years where he raised his daughter. He worked as a lawyer. Ray was overjoyed, a lawyer too! He couldn't believe his luck; it appeared as if they were sent to help him complete his mission.

They devised a plan to fake the sale of the resort and condominium to George. Once this was done, Ray could then sell the property for real, give the money in a good way and get it back 50 times.

Lily fell for it too. Ray had convinced her, using some complex banking terms, that they money would be available in a couple of months via the stock market. He regaled her with stories about what they were going to spend the money on, appealing to her greed. She believed him and signed over all of the property to George.

"The nun says you have to disappear now." Sandra told Ray. "We have arranged a job for you as a live in manager at our family hotel".

Ray and Lily moved their belongings to small rented apartment in Bangkok.

The Hotel

One day Ray just vanished out of Lily's life, telling her he had a new job far away. He was driven to a seaside resort by George, to the huge family hotel. It was a towering building of over 250 rooms in the centre of town, close to the beach.

George treated Ray like a son. He gave him some good clothes, bought him food and had arranged with the owners of the hotel to install him as an executive manager with his own living quarters. This included free laundry, a generous allowance at the restaurant and a meagre salary.

Ray was on cloud nine, he couldn't quite believe what was happening to him.

The owners of the hotel were on holiday in America when he arrived. The other senior manager was also a family member whom they had grown tired of and wanted out. Ray took her place and ended up sharing an office on the executive floor with George.

Over the next few weeks George taught Ray about managing a large hotel and continued to treat him like a son. He took him to hotelier meetings where he was the only foreigner and felt quite special. He was also introduced to the mayor and had his photo taken with him. Ray was also sent on day trips to various attractions around town, so that he would have a good knowledge of the local area to share with guests.

Ray was flabbergasted by the entire experience. One afternoon he was standing outside the hotel and three Iranian guests came to him smiling and shook his hand.

They didn't say anything, just walked on, but Ray was convinced he was in the right place and this was simply a sign from the universe congratulating him.

He was enjoying learning from George and all the attention he got. He'd never had much love from his own father and this felt genuine. On the weekends George would return to Bangkok to see his family, leaving Ray in charge of the hotel.

Ray learned the hotel was worth 550 million baht. This was exactly 50 times what he had given up. He felt all tingly inside and seemed as if he was walking on air.

He really was living the dream.

Sandra helped him to advertise the resort for sale through family friends on the island. "The nun says it will sell in a few weeks". They had a couple of month's leeway since Lily believed it would take that long for the money to come through.

The senior manager whom Ray had replaced was understandably upset that she'd lost her job and in retaliation had reported him to the immigration department. One day three undercover officers showed up at the hotel to check if he had a work visa. Of course Ray hadn't, so he thought quickly, like a Thai, and said to them it was in his room. They followed him to his room but he was able to get in quickly and lock the door behind him. They were angrily banging on the door whilst he phoned George. George came to his rescue and spoke with the immigration officers, assuring them that a work visa would be applied for. Ray was in a panic; he was well aware that other foreigners had been caught without a work visa and had been thrown in jail. He'd managed to escape though. Ray recalled a story from his teacher friends in Bangkok when the school was raided by immigration. They had to escape to the roof, climb down a ladder and into a waiting van to avoid being caught.

The owners of the hotel then returned from their holiday after a month. They were a younger Thai couple, cousins of George, who had also been raised in America. They arranged a work visa for Ray, not an easy process but it was successful. Ray and the managing director had to sign over 200 sheets of paper in order to gain a work visa.

During the application process they had Ray make them a website for the hotel.

The owners liked Ray. He had learnt quite a bit about the hotel from George and had been sending them a daily report by email whilst they were away. They came to the hotel once or twice a week for a meeting with him and George. They wanted him to learn the duties of all the hotel departments, with a view to him taking over the general manager duties when George retired. They spoke of giving him the hotel.

Ray loved it, he was deep in the holographic universe adventure, but he was also scared because of all the things he had done in order to get there -lieing and stealing to get money, tricking his wife. He started to doubt himself and what was going on. Was it all a big trick? In the holographic universe you have to question your moral values. It's not easy, though; but Ray truly believed he was on a mission to save humanity.

A buyer showed up for the resort and land on the island in the form on a Thai army general. Ray asked too much for it, though, and the sale fell through. Ray was kicking himself.

That's when things started to turn bad. Sandra was furious with him and said he'd lost everything.

By that time Lily had figured out what was going on and had moved back into the resort. A lengthy court battle then ensued which eventually saw an agreement reached that George and Lily would share the resort and land.

The owners of the hotel were very demanding and had Ray working very hard. He was exhausted and not accustomed to having someone boss him around and he began to hate it there. He much preferred his laid-back lifestyle of running his own business in his own way.

They were slave drivers, worked all their staff hard and paid them little.

Their moral values were entirely different to what Ray was accustomed to. Staff would steal from the hotel on a regular basis. Ray put this down to the fact that they were underpaid and to their love of manipulation. They worked so hard and many of them would have another job to make ends meet.

There were security cameras all over the hotel and one of Ray's duties was to check the cameras to help unravel the latest theft. Guests were often robbed there. The staff were very manipulative and rarely gave straight answers,

Ray became more and more disillusioned. Instead of getting on with his duties, he started to question everything.

Why was an industrial sized magnet being put on the water meter? Why were they staff treated so poorly?

How come they were paid less than what was written on their pay slip?

Why did they turn off all the smoke alarms and lock all the fire doors?

"You pay peanuts, you get monkeys." he would rant in his daily reports.

Ray felt out of his depth. The owners were not impressed with his attitude and sent him to stay in a temple.

The retreat

Ray shaved his hair off and became a monk at a meditation retreat. He stayed there for several months and learned that one of the steps towards enlightenment was indeed the ability to see the past, present and future.

He practised meditation every day and for while felt very good. On one occasion it felt like a light bulb had been turned on inside his head and he felt completely full of love, which was also one of the steps to enlightenment. It didn't last long, though. As soon as he stepped out of the temple into the real world, his mind started to fill up again. He felt good, though, and had a good contact with people whenever he went out for a walk.

Then one day Ray received a hammer blow in the form of a phone call. "Do you know who this is?" said an angry Thai man on the other end of the phone. "This is Sandra's husband.". Ray's world just fell apart then. He was distraught. The husband went on to tell him that they had a young son and that Sandra had lied to him about everything.

Sandra called him later to end their relationship, saying he had been "Dropped like a stone", only later to call him from another number to say she loved him.

George then showed up at the temple and ruefully admitted that his daughter had been fooling around with lots of other men. He, too, rarely spoke directly, preferring to tell stories in a vague reference to the matter in hand.

Ray was in pieces. He'd been lied to and tricked and he'd failed in his mission to save humanity. He was absolutely disgusted with himself.

George agreed to take him back to the hotel, this time as the night manager.

Ray didn't have anywhere else to go. He had no money, no home and no prospects; so he agreed, hoping that it might be possible to retrieve the situation.

The night manager

Ray was back at the hotel but things were not the same. The magical feeling he once had was now gone and he saw things in a different light.

He would notice how George would pick on certain members of staff; he was quite vindictive about it too. He absolutely hated the previous night manager who was an old Chinaman. "I feel like I'm dangling over the edge of cliff." he would say about his life at the hotel.

The warm feeling that Ray had was gone. He didn't want to be there anymore; he just wanted to find a big hole and crawl into it.

The night manager duties were quite interesting, though. The seaside resort offered lots of adult entertainment. Often guests would bring someone back with them to their room. Sometimes things would go wrong and this would provide some light entertainment, which gave Ray a welcome distraction from his woes.

On one occasion three Iranian tourists were on holiday for the first time. One of them looked particularly different. He wore a huge white cowboy hat and had big bulging eyes. He looked a bit like a horny version of Yosemite Sam from the famous old cartoons. Late one night Ray was asked to go to his room to help solve a dispute.

He'd inadvertently taken a Ladyboy back with him, thinking it was a lady. His two friends came out of their rooms and they had a debate in the corridor. The Ladyboy said he'd already tried to have sex with her five times "Would you like to see the condoms?" Ray didn't say anything. The one of his friends smiled and asked him "What is it you want to happen here?". The guy was clearly ashamed that he'd tried to have sex with a man dressed as a woman. It happens a lot in Thailand and is the source of much amusement.

Then another time George got very angry and sliced the tyres of a car that was illegally parked on the hotel terrace. It turned out that the vehicle belonged to one of the Thai guests who showed up wearing a t-shirt with a picture of a hand gun and the words "This is my glock, there are many like it but this one is mine.". This entirely summed up his mood; he looked furious. Since George had also arranged to have the police tow his car away, all the managers had to go with him to the car pound to help pacify the unfortunate angry young man.

Out of the blue, one day Ray received a phone call at the hotel from one of his old Swedish friends who had managed to track him down. This was the first contact he'd had with any of his old friends since his disappearing act. They went to drink a few beers at a bar in town that night.

Ray told him of his adventure as his friend looked at him with mouth agape. It helped to bring out certain feelings and realisations he had about the situation he was now in.

Back at the hotel Ray was quite drunk and wanted to vent his anger on George for all the lies his daughter had told him, lies that he'd supported. He went into George's room and swung a few punches that missed. Then he picked up the nearest object, a phone, and threw that at him which missed and smashed through the window. George called the police who showed up quickly and Ray was told he had to leave. It was 3am and he was homeless.

Ray remembered a lady he'd met at a coffee shop a few weeks before; she seemed nice and was running a business in the town. He called her and asked if she could help. Thankfully she agreed and Ray moved into her house.

The Honey

Rose was a remarkable woman. She was divorced with three children and owned three shops in the town selling bee products. She was very beautiful and had a kind nature.

She'd previously worked at a beauty salon where she got very sick from the chemicals being used there. Rose took medicine from several doctors at the hospital, but none of them were making her feel better. Then one day she met a beekeeper from the north of Thailand who suggested she try royal jelly. This did the trick; she was completely cured. Shortly after that she divorced from her wealthy Chinese husband and, with the money from the settlement, opened a shop selling bee products.

Ray was well looked after there and he made a website for Rose who would bring him food every day. She lived in a grand house with a shared swimming pool. It was a nice relaxing atmosphere that Ray needed, in order to recover and give time for his wounds to heal. He had a hard time coming to terms with what he'd been through and he felt terrible.

Rose did her best to understand. "Some Thai people just want you to believe them". Ray wondered if that was true about Sandra but had doubts because it had all seemed so real.

Rose was a terrific lady. She looked after the staff well at her three shops and still found time to take private kick boxing lessons. She'd almost died in that beauty salon and, since discovering the amazing healing power bees provide, was content selling their products.

One evening she told Ray something about the royal family and how they had the ability to meditate and speak to people through a higher plane of existence. Ray recalled a time when he was arguing with Lily about cultural differences. Later on he saw a vision of what appeared to be a princess wearing a beautiful white dress, covered in jewellery, smiling and saying to him "We like it this way.". Ray felt a shiver go down his spine again. There were mysteries that he just didn't understand, just like the music playing the bar that night on the island. He felt like a failure, but this was just the start of another adventure.

Ray was broke, he had nothing and, whilst it made him felt terribly afraid, there was also a tremendous sense of freedom.

The giks

After a few months Ray moved into a small, cheap apartment. His dear old grandmother had sent him some money that was just enough to live on.

The new apartment was quite a run-down old building but it had a swimming pool that he used every day. He'd lost a lot of weight, having eaten mostly Thai food and hardly drank alcohol at all.

With his new found sense of freedom he started to realise he was attractive to the opposite sex. Many ladies would stop to talk with him and, because he didn't have anything, he felt like he had nothing to lose.

During the 6 month stay at that old apartment Ray had a long line of lovers or giks as they are known in Thailand. They were just casual affairs for fun. Ray met Thai ladies from all walks of life. One was a senior manager he'd met through the hotel and she practically jumped into bed with him on the first night. She was a lovely woman who came from a Thai Chinese family.

There were many more, teachers, entrepreneurs, a lawyer, barista, accountants and a receptionist to name a few. Ray felt like James Bond. He was having a great time and was totally honest with the ladies he met. Some would show up with their car and ask Ray to drive them around to show the sights. From his experience as a hotel manager, he knew a lot of the nice spots to take them to. Sometimes it was a trip to a nearby island or to a temple or a quiet beach. Ray knew all the good places to go and the best restaurants too.

Some ladies took him away on holiday and paid for everything. Some gave him money and some gave him food and clothes. They really were like angels. It was a genuine pleasure to spend time with them.

Thailand has a fantastic atmosphere that is generated by the joy of life that the people have. It's geared up for living in the moment. A boat trip to an island costs as little as 50 pence and a good meal could be had for £1.

All this helped build his self-esteem. He was still troubled by the past, though, and occasionally he would get an angry phone call from Sandra's husband who would whine and complain a lot.

Ray had 12 lovers and could've had a lot more. He had over 50 phone numbers of ladies, all eager to spend time with him. He felt quite the stud but it was all getting a bit too much and he felt like it was time to move on.

He had one last thing that he needed to do before leaving, though. On that day Ray decided to have a homosexual experience with a Ladyboy. This was something Sienna had suggested he did but he felt too afraid at the time. Then Lily would tell him how Thai men cannot say they are men until they have had a sexual experience with a Ladyboy. Ray didn't like the experience and was relieved when it was over but later on felt glad he'd done it. He could understand the wisdom in doing it; a lot of the homophobic thoughts he had towards gay people dissipated. It was a worthwhile experience that helped to strengthen his character and, of course, gave his soul yet another emotional trip.

Return to village life.

One of Ray's lovers had taken a particular shine to him and would often drive to see him. Gayle was stunningly beautiful, clever and funny. She had previously worked as a school teacher.

They got along great and laughed a lot. Gayle had quite a temper, though, and a lot of suitors – she looked like a model. She assured Ray that she'd only ever had one Thai boyfriend and had never had a relationship with a foreigner.

Ray went with her to stay with her parents. Then later on she took him on a long drive up country to stay with her sister, who had married one of the poor Isaan famers.

Ray stayed at their house and, since the husband was the equivalent of the local mayor, he was treated with a lot of respect by the locals who nicknamed him the foreign mayor. It was a great place to stay.

Even the mayor gave up his bedroom for Ray and Gayle to sleep in.

The bedroom, though, was overrun with rats. Ray had a big problem with this and it would often wake him up at night with rats crawling all over the mosquito nets, desperately beating them away. In his resort Ray would lay traps for the rats and then let his cat eat them.

"You must make peace with the rats" Gayle said to him. "Let them sleep with you, it's OK." showing Ray how she let one of the rats sleep on her pillow. Ray didn't like the thought of it but stopped fighting with them. After a few days, the rats stopped coming.

Sienna had once taught him something similar about mosquitoes. "Make peace with the mosquito spirit in meditation; let them take what they need". Ray had done this too and the mosquitoes didn't bother him that much.

Ray was being treated like royalty in that village and was enjoying every moment. It was in stark contrast to his first visit to his now ex-wife's village.

Gayle told him how she and her sister had helped the husband become mayor by scaring the locals into voting for him. They used fake video cameras to make it look as if they were recording what they were doing at the voting station and this manipulated the vote in their favour. It was his wife who was doing most of the work, though, whilst he was enjoying spending time with the locals drinking whisky and talking.

A few weeks later it was Ray's 42nd birthday. On that day Gayle told him she was pregnant and that he was the father. Ray felt overjoyed and completely at peace.

There was something not quite right about the whole thing, though. Gayle would sometimes disappear in her car and one night Ray heard her sitting in the car screaming her head off at someone in English. "You f**king man, I want you to take a DNA test." She was getting quite carried away and shortly afterwards a storm broke out. There was lots of thunder, lightning, and rain. Then the power cut out. Ray went to the back door to retrieve his shoes. When he shone a torch on them two shiny black scorpions quickly scurried away. Gayle certainly knew how to whip up a storm; she was a Scorpio lady, too, funnily enough.

As usual, even though he was suspicious, Ray played along and started to make plans to provide for Gayle's baby. He contacted Sienna asking if he could help. He duly obliged and put him in touch with his sister in Hungary who would soon be opening a new resort.

Back to Europe

Ray said his goodbyes and flew into Austria where he was met by Sienna's sister, Ruth, and her husband, Roland. Ruth seemed genuine and friendly; Roland on the other hand wasn't very welcoming at all.

They didn't have a resort as Sienna had said, but were in the process of building a couple of extra rooms in their farm house in a small Hungarian village near the Austrian border. Ray wondered what he had let himself in for, but he had no need to worry as the universe had a plan for him.

He kept in touch with Gayle in Thailand and one day had a big argument with her. She went berserk and told him about all the other men she had been with, sending him photos of her with lots of different men. One was pointing at her stomach with a hand written sign saying "My baby.".

It was another Thai scam. Ray took a deep breath and once again felt that shiver go down his spine. It was a mix of disappointment and anger. The emotions from going up high and then going very low on the realisation it was all a big fantasy, were somewhat familiar now. It's the feelings your soul wants to experience in the holographic universe. Ray had certainly given his soul that experience to extreme levels.

At least he was back in Europe and not too far from home and his next journey would help him come to terms with his greatest fear.

Roland soon kicked him out and Ray was homeless again, this time with nowhere to sleep, no job and no money.

He took a train to Austria and made it to Eisenstaedt.

Once there, he walked through the town and a gust of wind and a small whirlwind brought into his path a woolly hat that he would later need.

He hitch hiked along the motorway heading east. Of course, it's not allowed in Europe as it is in Thailand, and the police soon picked him up. They were very friendly about it, though, and drove Ray to the nearest train station. "Just tell the conductor you have no money and they will let you travel to Vienna" the policeman smiled.

Ray made it to Vienna and sat in one of the parks asking passers-by if they could help him with some accommodation. It was a frightening prospect for him not having somewhere to sleep.

Someone suggested he go to a hostel not far from there. Ray had never been homeless before and queuing up outside the hostel, with smelly drunks and drug addicts, was not a pleasant experience. He walked away and came back later when the hostel was open only to find all the beds had been taken that night. The staff asked him why he was homeless and he told them "Well, I was staying with some friends but the husband wasn't happy about it." - which made the men laugh a lot. He was given a blanket and told he could sleep in one of Vienna's beautiful parks.

That night was one of the coldest and scariest nights of Ray's life. He couldn't sleep because he felt so cold. His body had adjusted to tropical temperatures and it was a shock to be in colder European climates. He would often get up to stamp his feet to keep warm and he kept nervously looking around, scared that someone might attack him. When he tried to sleep on a park bench he simply couldn't; it was far too cold and he was shivering. He could feel his heart beating very slowly as if it was about to stop. That was a very long night and he was relieved when the sun finally came up.

That day he walked across town to find somewhere warm to sleep. He knew he would die if he had to sleep outside again. The churches were locked and eventually he found an office that housed homeless refugees. They directed him to an EU hostel on the far side of the city. "You can take the tram there and nobody worries if you don't have a ticket here".

The EU hostel cost 1 euro for a bed in a warm room shared with over 50 others. Ray was very grateful for that and some of the Thai coins he had looked like a 2 euro coin, so he had some money to stay in the hostel for a few days. They also gave him a free breakfast and evening meal there.

During the days he would walk around Vienna. It's a beautiful city with a nice atmosphere, hardly any crime or violence. They have an old palace with fantastic landscaped gardens that Ray enjoyed walking around. It was in that park that he had the best contact he'd ever had with nature. Whilst standing in the woods, he was eating a bar of chocolate and a squirrel appeared in front of him and then climbed his leg, up his body and down his arm to eat out of his hand. Whilst this was happening a small bird perched on a branch nearby, was tweeting and jumping up and down. So Ray held his other hand out with some food and the bird ate out his other hand. He felt completely at peace with nature.

It had turned out to be a peaceful stay in Vienna, thoroughly recommended if you are homeless there. After a few weeks Ray felt that it was time to go home. He sent an email to some family members and his Uncle was kind enough to send him some money with which he bought a bus ticket and spent a night in a hotel where he had a good wash.

Finally home

Back in England Ray went directly to his father's home. His father's first reaction was to call the police. His wife calmed him down, though, and Sent Ray to stay in a nearby hotel that night. He was livid with Ray who had told him some of this story, but he could only understand it in a linear way.

The next day his Dad had calmed down, bought Ray a mobile phone and gave him some money. Ray stayed with one of his old friends for a few months. He was quite miserable, though, and hadn't fully understood or come to terms with what he'd been through. He still felt like a loser for failing in his mission to save humanity and spent a lot of time feeling sorry for himself. He felt different inside and found that he didn't have much in common with his old friends.

He made friends online with an angelic healer from Holland. She understood his situation and was very intuitive. A bit like Sienna, in touch with her soul, and instantly knew the best thing to do. "Go to this meeting in Glastonbury; there are lots of angels there who will help you." she suggested to him one day. Ray didn't have enough money to get into the meeting but was able to get a discount on the door. Once there he enjoyed a talk by a spiritual teacher who got the audience involved in some exercises that would help to develop them. She was very good too; Ray could understand that she was helping people find the balance of yin and yang inside of themselves. They were then asked to do exercises with the person sat next to them. That's when Ray met Dr Tina. She was a lovely woman from Scotland who was an NHS doctor on a sabbatical year. During one of the exercises Ray felt his soul beating for the very first time in his life. It's a bit like a heartbeat, only it's 1 inch to the right. Ray had a huge smile on his face and Tina invited him to stay with her for the remainder of her holiday.

He later went to stay with Tina in Scotland where he enjoyed spending time as a tourist, driving her nice convertible car and meeting her friends. Whilst there, he met up with two guys who used to drink in his bar in Thailand. One of them had married one of his staff and she was expecting their baby. Ray felt so happy he cried.

Tina took Ray on holiday to Holland. He had time to meet up with Sienna and have a chat. Of course Sienna instantly knew the right thing to say; "You will get it back 50 times in other worlds" which was a bit mystifying at the time but later became clear. "You're free now, free as the day you were born." Sienna enthused and went on to explain that fear and anxiety were Ray's biggest problems and now that he had faced them, his life would get a lot better. "You'll still feel afraid sometimes, but it won't overwhelm you any more". These were wise words indeed.

Tina's sabbatical year was coming to an end and she was going back to work soon. The fun times needed to stop since she worked very hard as a doctor. She arranged with some friends for Ray to visit one of the Holy Isles with a view to a permanent move. Ray stayed there for a few days and decided he didn't like it very much. It was a peaceful island that was owned by Buddhists, but he just didn't have a good feeling about it because he was still beating himself up inside.

Ray was homeless again and slept in the airport when he got back to England. Later he found an emergency night shelter and would sometimes sleep rough outside. It was very cold though. During the days Ray would spend time at a local internet café. He became quite friendly with the owners and made them a free website in exchange for a warm place to stay during the day.

After a few weeks Ray was given a room at a Salvation Army Hostel.

During his stay there Ray met quite a few interesting characters who had amazing stories to tell. It was quite a decent place to stay too; there was a snooker room with a full sized table and pool table, a computer room and a restaurant. They offered free breakfast and a heavily subsidised evening meal. He was assigned a support worker who took care of his needs.

One day at the internet café the owners asked him if he would like to help out and teach people there. Right away Ray felt his soul beating. That was the second time he had felt it in his life. As soon as he felt it, he knew he had to say yes.

Ray then asked at the Salvation Army if they could help him to find a teacher's course and they duly obliged. Ray attended a college course and passed, earning him a qualification in teaching adults.

Since then, Ray has made quite a few websites and taught even more people. He works and helps out at the internet café a couple of days a week and works from home. He enjoys his work a lot and finds it very satisfying. He also teaches on Skype and has helped Thai and Russian ladies to improve their English.

The Salvation Army helped him to move into a very grand flat on the top floor with a nice view of trees out of the front and back. It's similar to the flat he once owned and, soon after he moved in, he was given a lot of useful things such as a washing machine, refrigerator and cooker.

There are lots of blessings in his life. He couldn't see them for a while because he felt so ashamed at some of the things he'd done or not done. It was all in his mind. Some of the things that happened he's come to terms with and others are just meant to be a mystery.

Ray has discovered serenity in his life that he never had before. He's no longer waiting for the weekends and gets a lot of satisfaction in the work he does. He still feels bad sometimes; he's naturally moody and sensitive, so that's to be expected.

The relationship with his father has improved and he spends quality time with his grandmother. He has an interesting circle of friends, too, with a variety of age ranges from very different walks of life.

Ray came to the important realisation that it's the experience of the journey that matters the most and not so much the destination. Now he understands the importance of following his soul which communicates to him, either by beating or giving him a nice warm feeling in his heart. He stands up for that and is not afraid to speak out if someone tells him otherwise.

Needless to say, there are certain people who he used to know before he went travelling that are now afraid of him. You see there are two version of Ray, the timid, afraid one before he went travelling, and the version of Ray that exists now.

He feels good in his heart. He's still in the holographic universe and understands all he needs to do is say "yes" when his heart feels good and to be open to the opportunities that present themselves.

He's got some fantastic memories - which are why he felt compelled to write this story.

He certainly embraced his devil during those adventures and pushed the boundaries to the extreme. It's given him inner warmth that he delights in every day. Every night when his head hits the pillow he feels satisfied and grateful for his life.

He's also very sorry to anyone he may have upset during his adventures. It was never his intention to do that. Ray just had to follow his own path.

He'd also like to thank everyone involved and is very glad they crossed paths, even the ones who were doing badly, because all the experiences enriched Ray's soul and helped him to become a stronger person.

www.ingramcontent.com/pod-product-compliance
Lightning Source LLC
Chambersburg PA
CBHW050540300426
44113CB00012B/2194